Chill Relax and Car Flip

Kayne Frost

Table of Contents

Introduction

So, you've just heard of someone who sold their car for a decent profit, or maybe you've seen something like this on TV, or perhaps you're just interested in knowing the car flipping business. Well, I have good news for you: in this book you will learn everything about how to become a successful car flipper. Feel free to jump around the chapters if you only need to read certain topics. I didn't write this book like a story; rather, it's a manual for those who are wondering how the car flipping business works.

When I first started this business, I didn't own a car for over four years. Each week I drove a different car to work and either got a taxi, Uber or a co-worker to bring me back home. It was a fun experience driving so many types of cars and at the same time seeing what needed to be fixed before being sold. So just to let you know being in this business you'll be driving your cars a lot. The last thing you want to do is drive a personal car every day and only drive your selling car up the street or around the block only to find out that once it's been running for a period of time you notice some things that need attention and by that time you may have lost a potential buyer. Selling cars at work was common for me at the beginning. I had to work a nine to five job until my side business took off. So, during a lunch or a break I would meet a buyer in the parking lot and possibly sell a car right then and there. You never know when a buyer is going to call, and you don't want to miss it or go to voicemail. By the time you call that person back they may have already found another car they were interested in. The last thing you want to do is hold on to a car for longer than two weeks. This market is a depreciating asset and each day that goes by a new year comes and newer models come out. So, don't delay, stay sharp, and stay up on all new and used vehicles. The more you know, the wiser you look and the more confident you sound when presenting your sale.

But first thing is first, you need to get your feet wet. In this book I laid out all the things you will need to determine which paths to take. There are several and ALL make money! I want to make this book as short as possible, so let's get to it!

Knowing your cars and market

The best advice I can give you is to pick a car you or maybe a friend or family member knows very well. I would suggest picking a car you really liked, something you can get excited about building, buying and getting to know. Or even a high school car that you drove and maybe it had some problems that made you buy parts for it and you have a little mechanical experience on it. The point is to get familiar with one make and model really good before you try and learn every car out there. Trust me in today's time you can lose a lot of money and time because one type of car/SUV/ truck can have a variety of parts due to the maker having four or five makes for that model. Every bolt, every plug, the tiniest plastic pieces not lining up. can really throw you for a loop. They may look like that part fits on whatever picture you're looking at but until it's in your hands and you try to put it on you realize they are different. These types of problems could cost you days or weeks and you may lose valuable time in the process only to find out that you needed a different part.

Now the easiest way is to call a dealership and find out what part you specifically need (they will ask you for the last 8 digits of your VIN) but even the dealerships have caught on and will no longer give you this information for free over the telephone. You might have to go into a dealership and get this info in person but you can't do this often as even then they will catch onto you just using them to get the parts elsewhere and they will only give you the prices and if they have that part in stock or not.

They know the game just as you know. It's a tricky situation but if you buy every now and then from a dealership, they will give you this information freely. Like maybe some dealership transmission oil, or some special bolts you can't find anywhere but you need those that day or the next etc. Main thing is you don't want to be that person who just walks in asking for parts numbers.

Newer cars are always better to sell, but remember that there is a market for every car out there—you'd be surprised! If you're thinking about a car and really have no idea anything about it, you can always look on KBB.com Kelly Blue Book to get a rough idea what those cars are selling for, or you can punch in the year make and model on craigslist/auto trader and see what other people are selling those cars for. Again, it's a very rough estimate! People selling their personal vehicles always want much higher than the car is really worth. So, just because you see a car on a site selling really high, don't think you'll be able to sell your car just as high. They might have had that car listed for over six months and not realizing their asking price was too high. Usually, those people will end up selling their car really cheap in the last few weeks once they sold their house and are about to move. Sometimes people think if they list it high, they have a lot of negotiating room to come down when in reality people seeing their ad thinks this person is nuts and no one is ever going to call them. I have bought and sold four cars before while this other person was trying to sell their one car way too high. I sometimes use their high prices as an advantage to list mine cheap just to sell it and move on to the next. Depreciation is always against you in this market. The faster you move cars the better it is for you. People looking at cars on sites will see which cars are coming and going and which ones stay on a site for a very long time. Trust me, when you have a car longer than three weeks, people will text you saying they've seen your posting for a long time and will try to lowball you with cheap offers. People are always watching, and knowing you are in and out with your sales will make your confidence in your sales and you'll know when and how to play hardball when dealing with customers. You'll know what other people are selling, what other cars are your competition, and how much better (or worse) your car compares to others. This is big in the car flipping business! Knowing who your competition is, is key! People will try to lie and say there are other cars out there cheaper or better than yours, but if you really know your stuff, you can say with confidence, go and look at that other car and if you like it buy it. That alone lets the other person know you have a good vehicle. If they are really interested, they will either negotiate with you right there, or may even take off and will text or call you fifteen minutes later trying to negotiate with you on the price later. It will be up to you on what you want to sell it for, but don't take the bait right off the bat. You can seriously save hundreds of dollars by knowing your market and knowing your car's value!

Using your budget wisely

This is going to vary on everyone's financial status. I can tell you how to flip 100k into a successful business, a 50k profit into a good hobby, or even $1,000 into some quick cash like $300 extra bucks in your pocket to pay off some bills etc. When I first got into this game, I was intrigued with people who started off with a paperclip and worked simply off of trades as they worked themselves up to a car, a vacation, even a house. Anything is possible in the car flipping industry with any amount of money. But what people don't understand is that just because you have a lot of capital to start off with doesn't mean you can't fail in this market. No, you can make a lot of bad buying decisions and start to lose your money really quick.

I say the higher money you have to put in, the less troubled cars you should be buying. If you have 25k to throw in, I'd say look for cars that are selling for around 10k that need no work at all done to them. Maybe a little bit of interior cleaning and a good car detail on the exterior and it's ready for sale. Maybe a SUV or pickup. Buy one or two. But check the market on those cars before going all in. If you can make an easy $1,000 on each vehicle, multiply that times two. Then for something less than two weeks of waiting on the title to come in with your name, a 1-hour car cleaning, and a 1 hour of taking pictures and listing it, I'd say that's a pretty good profit. Now if you can make more like $1,500 or $2,000 per car even better! But if you have the money, I'd say go this route. I wouldn't buy 3 cars for $5,000 a piece that each car needs about $1k to 2k of work to get them in running condition. Even though it will still equal your budget limit, the turnaround time is going to be a lot longer. You may only be getting one car per month or even two months depending on how much work the body shop has ahead of you. The rewards might be better than the ones that don't need no work but the turnaround time is going to rely on something outside of your control. So even though you might make 3k or even 5k per car is it really worth it to make that money once per month? What if it's 2 months or 3 months later, is it still worth it? If you can manage both the quick cars and have a longer car on the side, then go ahead and do that. But don't rely on the big more problematic cars on your whole profit. This is where things get antsy and your temper starts to get tested.

Starting off with under 10k is possible but I strongly suggest you have another source of income to keep you afloat until you hit the 20k mark. You can still buy some decent cars under 8 years old that will make 2-3k profit. It won't be a simple car wash and vacuum, but it will involve some body work and possible engine work needed. Maybe a new throttle body, a new radiator, some brakes or one side suspension. Maybe you'll need to replace a bumper, a fender, some headlights, or even a hood. These are still good profitable cars but will need some work done to them. I know a lot of people who start off in this category. It's a great way to make some side money or expand a startup business.

Starting off below $5k. This is where I strongly suggest you know a good bit of cars to make a decent profit. Honestly speaking, don't go in thinking you can buy a $1,000 car and make $1,000 the next day. There have been some rare instances where someone won a $800 car and sold it the next day for $1,800 but what that person failed to tell was, there were 20 cars of the same make and model that day. There was a rainstorm that delayed the auction for a few hours and a lot of people went home after waiting over an hour thinking the auction was over, and that rain gave some light hail damage to the cars. While it is possible, it's super rare to get these golden deals. I mean I've seen deals go through where the car in line that the auctioneer is standing in front of, is different than the picture posted where the auctioneer is going off of and thinks they are selling, the person who wins it either gets a smoking deal, or they just got burned whenever the mix-up gets settled. Sometimes they will rerun that car at the end of the auction but I have seen some cars that were going for $4000 and the one mix-up car gets sold for $500 because everyone thought a 1980 car was being sold and someone took a gamble and won a car really cheap. Does it happen, yes. Is it often? No. Cars that you buy for $800 etc. will come with all sorts of surprises. It may start, it may pull forward, but you really never know the full scope until you get it past 40 mph. Then the real problems start to kick in. Will the engine overheat? Will the transmission slip? Will there be electrical problems? I have bought these cars because I got dropped off at an auction an needed a ride back home and instead of paying a taxi/Uber/lyft, I thought I'd make at least $200 for wasting my time and coming up empty handed, because at the end of the day I want to make some sort of profit even if it's $200. When I bought this car it was a standard, no power steering, no power windows, grease in the front seats like a mechanic owned it. But guess what, it got me home. It was a really crappy car and cleaning it wasn't going to make it any better. I vacuumed it, washed it and listed it. I listed it for $1,100. The questions I got were hilarious! I would get questions like, How's the A/C? Does it have power windows? How's the radio? I always replied with the same answer: "It's a $1,000 car. What do you expect?" I even put in the ad: "This is a great car if you are looking to skip the bus and drive to work." What I learned was no matter what price you list a car for, people always want something not realistic.

The cheapest cars can be some of the costliest vehicles to get back into shape. These are not going to be the big deal investments. Even if you are an ace mechanic, you'll still have to put in hours to get something to work. I used to know a mechanic who would thrive on the under 2k cars that needed work. These cars usually needed rebuilt transmissions or engines. He would end up making a good profit like $3,000 but again he had to put in his own hours that normally he would be sharing with someone else. So, if he had no work, he could work on one of these cars. So, in actuality he was filling in his dead time had he been a successful mechanic with a busy workshop. We are all not going to have this expertise level of skill. If you have it and want to dabble in it so see how it works, go ahead. My advice is to save up more money and buy a better car that doesn't need so much work

If you don't have $5k to start off with and are really wanting to invest $1,200 to $2,000 because you really need the money, all hope is not lost. I would suggest you look into buying a city car. These will be basic cars but will be extremely maintenance and well-kept mechanically, so these will be Chevy Lumina, S-10 truck, Ford Taurus or something along those lines. They are usually all white and may even have an amber light on top of the vehicle. They might be a little muddy/ dirty depending on what that car was used for, but again these cars will have good A/C, good brakes, good steering, good suspension etc. The looks may not be that great, but they'll drive well. You might have to do some normal cleaning on it, and you more than likely might have to do some small touch up paint around the vehicle from rock chips or even some paint flaking in some cases. They will have a clean title and sometimes, I repeat sometimes low miles. Usually the low miles sell for much higher, but it's usually over 150k miles. Look up those cars and find out what they are selling for. See if you can get it for a certain price and sell it for at least a $300-$500 profit. These cars aren't going to make you $1,000, but they will make a profit. I once bought a 2007 Pontiac G7 for $1,300, went and picked it up and it drove like a dream. Everyone was selling them for $2,200 and I listed it for $2,000. Ended up selling for $1,900 in about two days. So, something that took me a couple of hours to get, an hour of cleaning and taking pictures, it brought me an easy $500 minus the $100 for the title transfer. I didn't expect much because I knew the market wasn't that great for it. But I had nothing else going on and saw a quick opportunity to make some quick money and jumped on it. Every car has a profit potential, you just have to search for them and find them.

Buying a Salvage Title vs Clean Title

Buying a clean title is the easiest route to go if you just want to test the waters in the car flipping business, but it will also be the most expensive one on the auction-day lot. Why? Because everyone else is thinking the same thing as you. Dealers like to go for clean titles because they will make their money in financing and will see their returns in the long run. You are just a quick-flip person, and all you want to do is clean the auction lettering from the windows, maybe top off the fluids, vacuum the inside, and give the car a good detail. You just want to wash it thoroughly, take pictures of it, and list it. The thing about clean titles is that you make very little profit on them unless you have a buyer in mind already or you recognize a certain year, make, and model number that might give you an advantage over others in selling the car for a higher value. These circumstances are rare, but they can happen. Flipping a clean title car is the best way to go if you just want to get a feel for things.

Now flipping a car with issues is even better. Even if it is a clean title (not wrecked or flooded), chances are it's never been involved in an accident, but it may have some electrical or mechanical issues. Depending on your knowledge, you may or may not want to get involved with one of these cars. I like to stick to cars that I know. That doesn't mean that I know every year make and model out there, but there are some cars that are so similar in parts that you can know just one really well and actually know about four more that are practically the same. Currently, I've been dealing with Dodge Chargers. Dodge Challengers, Chargers, and Chrysler 300's all basically use the same subframe, just different exterior parts. This can also be said of Lexus and Toyota, Chevy and GMC, etc. They all use very similar makes and just name them differently, like the Chevy Colorado and the GMC Sierra.

The tricky thing about jumping around from different years and makes is that although the part may look similar, it may have a different plug end, or the bolt hole might be a little off. With a little bit of mechanical knowledge, you can always make something work when it's really close. So, if you want to dabble in cars with problems, then I suggest you pick a car you like and try to buy a lot of similar cars, so you can get the hang of things for that one particular model. You don't want to buy all kinds of different years and makes only to be frustrated when every car requires different parts from several used car-part places and even outrageous dealerships. This can become very costly and time-consuming when you don't know what you're doing. If you get into a particular car and find that locating parts is becoming too problematic, then I would sell that car as soon as possible and move on to another. I've had several instances where there was a car that was just too good to pass up, and I ended up spending a lot of money hiring several mechanics trying to locate a part for that car. And foreign and domestic cars can vary in price. For example, for German cars you will need to find a German car mechanic who knows what he's doing. Most mechanics will say they know how to work on things just to tear your car apart and ultimately leave you with the same problem you started off with, but now your car's in pieces, and you have to find another mechanic, gather all of your parts, and move to another location. The cycle goes on and on. If you are experienced with foreign cars, then by all means get into that market. But I would stick with domestic cars at first. I've had several friends buy BMW, Mercedes, etc. only to have those cars sitting around for two or more years with new engines, computers, etc. and still no resolution to the initial problem.

Once you get good at dealing with problem cars, you can visually check for things like faulty wiring, spark plugs, coils, starting problems, a car shaking problem, an engine issue, etc. You will become more experienced the more you fix these cars and come across these initial issues. You can check these cars out at the auction and see if you want to gamble on fixing that car. Be careful, because some people will intentionally pull a plug wire or a fuse out to make a car seem like it has issues when they are pre-inspecting vehicles at the auction. They are hoping that this will scare away or discourage buyers from bidding on that car so they can get it for a cheaper price. Most of the time, the auctioneers will pull the car because they know it was running fine when they drove it in and therefore know someone has messed with it. Other times they won't be keeping track, and it will get sold to someone who was pulling some shady stuff. The good thing about learning this side is that it gets you basic knowledge about the mechanical and electrical parts very quickly. You might have to pay a little bit more because you're not fully aware of what's going on, but as time goes on, you'll start to figure out what could be some common issues. That way, when you have to take it to a mechanic, you'll know if they're trying to scam you or not. Do you really need an oil filter for a rear main seal leak? You'll ask, "What does an oil change have to do with a transmission fluid change?" Sometimes, mechanics will say things just to test your knowledge.

Now comes the fun! Buying a badly wrecked car or a salvage title. Let's go over the basics. A salvage title is when an insurance company has declared a car a total loss—that its repair would cost more than its original estimated value. So instead of paying a mechanic, electrician, or body shop, they'd rather total out the car, pay the first owner the blue book value, and sell the car as a salvage title. They want to try to get whatever they can and cut their losses. They don't care if they get $100 for it; the way they see it, it's a salvage, and it's the next person's headache. Some locations will sell a car that should've been totaled and been declared a salvage title, but that person or company decided not to claim it as a loss and will sell it as a clean title. It's still going to be a battle getting that car back into roadworthy condition, and it doesn't change the stakes any. But people do like to buy a clean title over a salvage title any day of the week. The thing about a salvage title is that it is usually illegal to drive in any state while it is still in salvage condition. The state will not issue you any temporary tag for it, some insurance companies will not insure it, and it will be hard to find anyone to finance it. You must get it into a restored salvage title or a rebuilt title before you can get those things. Some states will require you to get it inspected by a registered state car inspection shop; other states will require you to bring it in so a state trooper can look at the car thoroughly, looking underneath with a mirror for any repaired frame damage, etc., opening the hood, checking the frame and suspension, making sure all the turn signals work, horn, lights, etc. Not many states will look at the airbag or ABS light. Mainly, the check engine light has to be off, and the car must pass some basic inspection tests before it is considered roadworthy again. Last, some states just don't care about any of this and will put it back to a rebuilt state without any inspection. I've heard of people taking cars that didn't pass in their own state to a friend or relative in another state just to get the title converted. I would never try to sell a car in a salvage state without getting it to a rebuilt or restored title state. In some places, like New York, it is very hard and you have to provide all kinds of documents on who's worked on your car, and if you are ever trying to sell your car on a national level you will lose a lot of buyers who don't want to hassle with a car that is fixed but without proof of who fixed it because then they still have to get it converted to a restored title state.

Benefits of Restoring a Salvage Title

Once you've figured out your states restoring salvage title process and figured out if you want to dabble in this area this can be one of the most profitable sections to make money in. Not a whole lot of people want to get into the really bad wrecked cars, or don't even want to leave the clean title area just because they don't think there's money to be made in this field. I'm here to tell you that 75% of cars I sell were once salvage vehicles. The profit margins can range from $4000-$15,000 off one car. It could even be higher depending on the car being fixed and or sold. The main thing is locating a good car rebuilder.

The first thing you're going to run into is the experience and or knowledge of the damage that needs to be repaired. I have written in this book about sticking to certain makes and models so you can get to know one specific car and become an expert in that car before you move on to another one. Starting off buying 3 bad wrecked cars because they were cheap, can leave you in an inexperienced field and possibly give up car flipping not requiring the basics first. Cars today are made of mostly aluminum and they bend and crease easily. So, when you see a car that was wrecked bad it may just be the exterior pieces that can be easily replaced. Like a hood, a fender, a bumper, or even a quarter panel. Believe it or not but a lot of used car places sell sections off a car for these specific reasons. They know there is a huge market in the rebuilt title field. Now the newer the car the harder it is going to find that part. It may be available but being so new these parts will be pricey. A quarter panel off a new car from that year can go for about $4,000. Whereas that same part in about 2 years will be about $600. So no, newer isn't always better in the restoring field. When you do know your cars and know there are other models similar to yours, you can shop around and find those frame parts etc. at local junk yards or online used car places like car-part.com. Don't be afraid if the part is far away. Most of these places do ship. I wouldn't ship anything bigger than a hood, but a door, bumper, wheel etc. I would.

Frame damage is going to be the root cause of most salvage vehicles. So, you'll first have to know of a frame puller who can pull the frame back into place before you buy a frame damaged car. No, not all body shops are frame pullers. I'd say about 80% of body shops are just regular small damage repair and paint only. Then when you do find one, make sure you find another to price shop, or compete against each other for the best price. Again, you might have to buy that section of the frame from a used car parts store once you bring them your car. That's the other thing, you are going to be the go-fer boy when it comes to repairing your car. You want to be involved in everything that is going on. You do not want them to replace everything that's needed. If you ever do this, you are basically giving them an open checkbook or handing over your credit card and telling them to do whatever it takes. This will show you have no idea what you're doing and it's okay for them to take advantage of you. But if you are working at a regular 8-5 job, be prepared to get a part from a local part store during your lunch break and take it to that shop working on your car. The problem is once they start working on your car you don't want them to delay because you didn't get them the part in time. If you had experience you could save hundreds of dollars by ordering from places like Rock auto and having them shipped a week before you bring them your car. The more parts you have ready for them, the faster and less inconvenienced you'll be having everything ready. If you do slack off, your car can get pushed back a day or two and you'll ask what happened and why are they taking longer but they'll say they couldn't work on it when they didn't have the parts and they have other cars. Try to go up there as often as you can to see where they are at with working on your car. The less you show your face the less they think it's a priority to you. You will not be bothering them stopping by for 2 or 3 minutes just saying hello and checking in

The benefits of the restored title industry are the profit to be made. The way I've always looked at it is, some people don't have the 30 or 50k to buy the newest model, but they do have $15k for a restored title that looks the same as the new car. Yes, it will have a branded title, but who is going to know when you're driving down the freeway at 70mph, or you're sitting at the streetlight? Is anyone going to come up to your window and ask you what type of title it is? No, they aren't. People who know about restored titles usually have bought them before and they already know what they are getting into. It's your job as a seller to make the car as new as possible to get more money for it. The less you put in, the less you can ask for it. You will never make the new prices or let's say just only 5k off from a new car. Don't be greedy. Buyers would rather pay the extra 5k to get new with warranty and a clean title. Your goal is to put about 3k-6k into it total and sell it for a profit

Replacing airbags will be optional. Most states don't require this when passing inspection, but it's more of a safety issue when you're selling to other people. Replacing airbags will require you to have to reset the whole system afterwards. There is never a guarantee they will deploy again if involved in a serious accident. This is why insurance companies will only cover liability and not full coverage when it comes to a rebuilt title.

Dealer auctions vs Public Auctions

Both of these have their own perks followed by a bunch of Do's and Don'ts. I'm going to have to combine them into one as it's best to describe both as a side by side comparison. First understand as I have mentioned in this book several times that car dealers are some of the shadiest people (including me). There are times you really want a sale to go down and with the car in interest already having so many question marks for a potential buyer to buy, you're not going to mention that the glove box doesn't shut right, or the center console lid doesn't properly shut sometimes. No, you'll be quiet just to get the sale when 10 other people have shown up and left and you have a person who just may buy and you don't want a final straw that drives that person away. So, when I say all dealers are shady, I mean they all are. Maybe you have never had an experience, but you know people who have. So, let's get to it!

I have been to many car dealers and public auctions and I have to say my best car buys come from public auctions. Meaning they are local tow yards, repos, found abandoned, previous owners arrested etc. Most of the time these will have markings on the windows and you might be able to see these in the pictures they posted, if not you may have to jot down the ones you are interested in and go down and view them in person. A lot of the time the staff working at these places have no idea on the condition or mechanical needs, so you'll have to use your best judgement or bring a friend who is a body guy or mechanic to give you some pointers. Sometimes these yards will have a "start the vehicle the day" before the auction but not start the car on the day of the auction because it's online only. I would strongly suggest you go and try to start these vehicles up. Plus, you can see the full condition of the car close up. Some of these places will take pictures in a way so you don't see the extent of the damage, or if there is even any damage at all. I have won cars online and shown up only to find out one side of the car was completely wrecked and the profit I had in mind shrunk instantly! Luckily that car was unable to start after they had described the car as in starting condition. So, they asked if I wanted it towed to my place for free or get my money back. I quickly took my money back. Funny thing was they listed that same car with the same pictures and listed it as a non-runner and sold even higher than what I won it for. Also, during the start time, you won't know if it has a bad transmission, bad suspension, bad steering. You might be able to put it in gear, but you won't be able to drive it. You won't know this until you have paid for it and they give you the keys. So, if you do win a car from one of these places and you get an idea of what might be wrong, never underestimate what you can't see. It's a gamble we all take, and you just have to hope for these best. I've bought a car that said it didn't start and all it was, was a battery cable that was cut. I wired it there on the spot and drove off. Sold that car the next day. But when you are checking the cars on preview day make sure you test everything. Windows, turn signals, A/C, radio, all the basic stuff. Because these are all simple things every buyer is going to do to you once it's in your possession.

I like Public auctions better because depending on the accident you can see you have a general idea of why that car is there. Or if it says Arrested and you know that person got arrested on the spot, got their car impounded and couldn't pay for the tow yards storage fees, so now that tow yard is trying to make up for any losses, they can recover. Now if the car says abandoned, then who knows what's wrong with the car. Did the transmission or motor lock and the owner said F it and tell the dealer they can come get it? Was it left in some apartment parking lot and then got towed away if the owner died, went to jail or left the state? It can get really dicey and these deals can look really promising but a rebuilt motor isn't cheap. That can range anywhere from $600 - $3000. Your profits can go up in smoke really fast. Another tricky situation is where they list the car as having no key for it and no markings on the windshield. It's a head scratcher for sure. Those always pique my interest and I will always write those down to go and take a look at and if the market is right for them, I will definitely put a bid in. I've lucked out on some of these cars and all it needed was a key made for $100 and a new battery. I've got some amazing deals this way, but I have also had friends who have bought these cars and once they got the key made, they found out the head gaskets were blown and the fix on that was an easy $600 immediately lost.

Most city vehicles are sold at public auctions. Some are sold at dealer auctions, but most can be found by a third-party site like Public Surplus or GovDeals.com. You can always contact a local city you have interest in and talk to the fleet manager and ask them where they post their vehicles for sale. It's free information so it's nothing that's bothering them. It's usually the same person who answers any questions regarding the vehicle's condition if that third-party website has their vehicles for sale. City vehicles are some of the best condition vehicles out there. Understand that a city usually has their own garage, their own mechanics and maintenance of their vehicles every 5000 miles. They are not like regular car owners where a person can overlook something for the time being. Nope, city vehicles are used every day and a small problem can turn into something big later. So, they got to fix things right away. Plus, the city will have a blank check when it comes to fixing cars. Once a car has gone past a certain mileage or once it has been repaired an X amount of times is when they decide to retire that car for sale. They won't fix any problems before they sell it. When it comes time for the regular maintenance schedule, they will just send it to the decommission yard and someone will go remove all the emergency equipment and the next phase will be to call the third party company to come and take pictures. The good thing is all of the fluids will be topped off, most of the time have good tires, wipers, etc. (all depending how long the cars have been on the yard before selling) The good thing about city cars is they'll have a good description of what was wrong before they send the car to be sold. If it has a bad motor, transmission, a leak, bad A/C, unknown electrical issues etc. those will be listed in the description. On dealer auctions everything is usually listed as unknown mechanical issues.

Public hosting sites are going to each have their own feedback ratings. Some people will have good relations, and some will not. With everything going online, I hate to say this, but some of these small auction companies will use shill bidders against their own sales. I have witnessed it and find it frustrating when trying to buy cars from that place. You can find out using the auction's terms and conditions of bidding. When you become the highest winner, you will have less than 5 days to make payment. If you don't, they will call you and tell you will be banned from their site if you don't pay off that vehicle. Now you will see another bidder's ID who outbid you on a couple of cars and has won, the next auction that they hold those same cars will be relisted and the same buyer is bidding on other vehicles. Did they get banned? When you win a car from a dealer or public auction all sales are final. It is extremely hard to get your money back. I've won a car that was listed as a V8 and it ended up being a V6 and was told I should've come and previewed the car beforehand. They ended up giving me a few hundred bucks back, but it is hard to get any money back. Each site will have their own customer relations etc. It's a good idea to look at the feedback of a site before you bid. I have my favorite spots as these people will work with me on things not listed etc. This kind of stuff goes a long way when you're spending thousands of dollars there. Things that go unwritten when they are obvious in person and how the auction responds to your situation, you'll know who you want to deal with etc. in the future. You'll just have to get out there and experience these things for yourself

Dealer auctions are the worst! First, you're dealing with all of the other shady dealers out there. Every dealer is selling their crap cars to each other. Let me tell you how it works. Car dealer auctions are usually grouped in how many cars are brought in by one dealer. So, it's usually the big dealers who are on the premium lines, or their first cars to run through the line during auction day. So, every small dealer has eyes on these lines in particular. Now here's the tricky situation, these places will be running 3-5 lanes at the same time. So, while the big dealers are getting all of the action, the small dealers are hardly getting any action. Most of the small dealer cars will get passed on because they are asking too much for them. Back to the "good dealers" here's what the small dealers are hoping for. They are hoping that Ford, Toyota, Lexus are bringing in the used car trade-ins that the dealer doesn't want on their lot and sends those vehicles straight to the auction to get whatever they can get. That big dealer is going to make money off the finance charges on the new car they just sold so the trade in is whatever. The small dealers know this isn't shady trying to sell back to shady dealers. It's basically a new car untouched by small dealers and only has a couple of owners when it hits the dealer auctions. Big dealers like Chevrolet, Dodge etc. won't do a trade in on a very old car. They'll do something of value to get a small profit from the auction so it's not like the small dealers are buying crap cars. It's once a small dealer has gone through several owners it then becomes a thrashed car. So, while we're on the topic let's see why the small dealers get their cars passed on. It's because they first bought that car on the good premium line (paid a premium price too) and then made 5x their profit, the car has been wrecked a few times, has had multiple parts repaired, interior is dirty etc. then they figure they've made well above their investment they'll just throw it back into the auction to get whatever they can get for it (basically like a known dealership only on a much worse scale). Usually, when that car has become a problem for them, they don't want to put more money into it and they try to resell it. They might have bought the car initially for 20k, but 3 years later and 100k miles added they are seeking 10k for it. When that same car is listed locally by a private seller for 9k. These guys are just being greedy and want every penny even after they have already made 15k in profit and selling it for just 5k they would be making a total of 20k on the car total in finance charges. And who wants to buy a car with over 5 owners when you can buy the same model with less wear and tear and less money from a one or two owner car. It makes no sense, but these guys will do this until someone buys that car for somewhere around their high price.

Dealer auctions are good because they do drive them when going through the lanes. So, if they are leaking, smoking, rattling, act you can see this in real time. If you are home and bidding online, you won't be able to see this. I tell you this because I once took a gamble on a car for $1000 when that car was being sold for 4k locally, when I went to pick it up it had an obvious knock in the motor. I didn't even get down the block before the car died and overheated. Again, all sales are AS IS and I was stuck like chuck. I have been to preview days at these auctions and have tested these cars in similar situations and people end up paying high when they are bidding online, not knowing otherwise. Once I started up a classic car because it looked to cool with a blower on it and the keys inside. It was early in the morning, no one was out there, and I wanted to hear it fire up. I got it to start without a jump and it had a big knock in the motor. Before I had left that day, they had removed the keys and weren't letting anyone start it. I believe two other people tried to start it and it was an obvious noise heard from far away. That car had brought a lot of buyers interested in that car. Crazy thing was when it was time to drive it through the line, they still didn't start it and had a bunch of employees pushing it from the rear. The auctioneer just listed all the work done to it and it was a long custom list. At the end the auctioneer said, "Man this is an exciting car, and I know a whole bunch of you are interested in it. It sounds like this thing can move, so let's start the bidding at X." The car ended up selling for over 30k and I bet the buyer thought the motor was in good condition and it was just a starter or dead battery is why they didn't start it. The auctioneer never did mention it had a knock in the motor. So be sure you check these cars out in person if possible. Know that if you don't, you're going to the casino and hoping for the best. Side note: Be weary for sellers bidding against their own cars to raise the price. You'll only know through whispered voices.

Wrecked cars at the dealer auctions are the safe bet. You can determine the wrecked parts and calculate how much it's going to cost to repair and look at what the going market is and see if you want to place a bid on it. Most dealers don't want to waste time on wrecked cars because it takes a lot of time for the repair process and they are more interested in selling volume than one big profit. Plus, if a car is a salvage most dealers will not be able to finance it. It will have to be a cash out deal. As of writing this, I don't know every state's insurance policy on salvage or rebuilt titles but from the few states I've lived in, restored salvage titles can only get liability, not full coverage. So, if you're not looking for a finance profit and just want a quick flip profit wrecked car at the dealer's auctions can go pretty cheap. Only when the cars are within a year or two do used car dealers want a piece of the pie. These cars will have less than 10k miles and will come straight from the big dealer with one owner. But they will have 4-5-year-old cars that most dealers will stay away from but can still bring you in 5-10k profit.

Benefits of buying out of state vehicles

Everyone wants to buy local so they have the benefit of inspecting the vehicle in person. Buying out of state is extremely risky but can also be the most rewarding. With so many auctions being held daily across the country, not every dealer can participate at each and every one. The person who takes the time to go through all of the upcoming auction lists will have the benefit over others and see what's out there. Yes, most auction sites do have a search bar to look up certain vehicles, but there are also many typos where the auctioneers make mistakes on listing the vehicle. So instead of properly listing a Ford Crown Victoria, their listing might be Ford CrownVictoria. So, you will miss out on your search, unless you took the time to go through every vehicle in the list. These are gems to find. You can always add these cars to your watch list and have them notify you when these vehicles come up. You might have to be logged in so you can hear the chime bell.

Another reason people don't buy from out of state is they are unaware of shipping transportation companies they can use to get your car to you without having to drive all the way out there. You have to check the auction's rules because sometimes they want you to pay in person, and if you're 800 miles away, that's going to throw a wrench in your situation because now you can't schedule a driver to pick up your vehicle. I've had this done to me several times, but the thing was they never did list that information. It was only when I was trying to pay, that they told me I had to pay in person. What usually happens is I cancel the deal and they relist the car. But it's always a hassle because both the seller and you have to email and contact the auctioneer to let them know, you both agreed to cancel the bid because if you don't the website's automated response will auto ban you after 5 days of non-payment. It sucks because you might've gotten a great deal. If the car is within a reasonable driving distance, I'll make plans to go and pick it up myself. It's only when the miles are 1000 away plus is when I'm not really set on driving for the next 5 days to go and pick up this vehicle.

Good deals can come from far and hidden spots. When there is an auction being held in the middle of nowhere the chances of those cars going cheap are going to be high. You might have to pay extra to a driver to go out of their way (like over three hours) just to go get it, but it is possible. So, if the car is 100 miles away a car from the nearest major city, add another $300 on top of it so drivers can be willing to go pick it up for you. You can always start off small in your shipping price range, but if the auction place has a 5-day window pick up, then you really have no time to sit around and wait for the best deal in the auto transport industry. You'll have to put it out their high up front to get noticed right away and get priority on your pick-up date. Otherwise, you could possibly lose your paid car back to the city.

The downside of buying vehicles out of state is you have to rely totally on the description listing. And those are always a 50/50 accuracy. You can hope what that auctioneer listed was true but if it wasn't then you really can't do anything about it. You won't know the full story of the car until after you have paid for it and have paid for the transport, plus all the time it took to get to you. Even if the auctioneer agrees with you for whatever reason you say they listed the car under a false pretense, they won't reimburse you for the shipping etc. You'll have to pay for the transportation to get it back. If you think about suing etc., you'll be in an uphill battle. There are risks when buying out of state, but those are the same risks you are buying in state too. Most places sell their vehicles AS IS. It doesn't matter if they didn't disclose something or didn't list something properly. It's the risk we all take. Now given that info, you are less likely to run into bad situations more than good ones. But I'm just stating they are nearly impossible to ever encounter while being in this business. I probably run into at least one per year, and that is pretty good odds.

The luxury of being able to get a trailer, a friend to go with to drive your car back or setting up a local wrecker is far better to most folks than to go down the hassle to getting a car delivered several miles away. But being able to broaden your search to nearly all of North America helps you out in the long run. The more you get familiarized with the out of state process the easier it becomes. The more you'll know about the average shipping charges from various states so you can determine the profit margin when bidding on your car. Or if you have good relations with a certain shipping company you can call them directly before an auction starts to find out how much a car will cost to get it to you. The possibilities are endless and going this route you'll never be empty handed. In fact, you'll probably get more frustrated seeing so many good deals go by as you won't be able to buy everything you see. And that is only going to drive you to move faster, get your cars done quicker, and sell as soon as possible

How to buy a used car just for a flip

As I've talked about the people who use this to their advantage and prey on people's financial abilities, I am not a fan of that nor did I write this book for you to do that. But I do know that when people sell cars, it's only for a few reasons. Reason one, they have no use for it anymore. Reason two: they've had multiple issues with this car and they don't want to put any more money into it. Reason three, they fell on hard times and are in need of any money possible and selling their transportation is a good boost to their financial situation.

When they have no use for it, it's usually a good sign. Maybe they bought a new car, have too many toys, or there was a dearth in the family and that was a relatively deceased car. These cars are usually in decent running condition and need little to get them up and running to a selling state. Basic things to check are, fluid leaks underneath, does the A/C work, is it cold? Does the heater work? Do all the doors open properly? Do all of the windows roll up and down? Is there any noticeable body damage, or frame damage under the car or inside the engine bay? Do the headlights, wipers, turn signals, and horn work? Does the radio work? Can you drive it around the block? Can you get it on the highway or above 50 mph without any gear slips or weird noises? Leave the car running for about 10 min after you took it for a test drive to see if it overheats. Do all of the gears shift properly, even reverse? Brakes good, no noise when coming to a stop? No pulls to the right or left when driving or coming to a stop? Do the tires have good tread? Does the car smoke when starting up? Does the car smoke while running? Black smoke is oil burning, and white smoke is poor engine compression/ engine failure. Does it idle smoothly? Does it run rough? These are some of the basic things to check out when overlooking a car in good condition.

If they've had multiple issues with this car or don't know anything about it, it'll be up to you to know what you're doing in this situation. I'd say at least try to get power to it and hopefully it turns over. That alone will make a big difference. If you can't get power to it, you won't be able to run a code scanner to the OBDII connector. You won't be able to see the miles, dash lights if any. This may be just a battery issue, or it may be a wiring issue. Rarely it's a blown fuse or bad relay. A bad fuse or relay should still get you power to the dashboard. I'd suggest you bring a portable jump box with you fully charged so you can hook it up to the battery terminals to see if it's just a bad battery. If you're able to get the car to turn over, that's a good sign. At least the motor isn't locked. If the motor doesn't turn at all you risk having a bad motor or even a bad starter. If the car turns over and doesn't start then it could be fuel, spark, or compression. That will have to be determined once you decide to buy it or not and run some diagnostics at your shop/house/ garage. If you are able to get the car to start and it does run, if it runs poorly then it could be a host of things starting with the same thing fuel, spark and engine combustion. But a running car is always better than a non-running car. You're talking about a person being able to sell a car for $5000 in running condition to a $2000 car in non-running condition.

When someone is selling a car for personal reasons, then that car is usually a good car to buy. You have to make sure you run through all of the basic tests before buying it. You have to make sure they have the title in hand and they don't owe any money on it. You have to make sure there are no title loans on it or no bank liens. When people are desperate, they won't tell you everything about their situation so they may be hiding some things that involve undisclosed paperwork. It will be up to you to find out everything before you hand over any form of payment to them. I would suggest you get a copy of the title with a phone picture and run down to the DMV to make sure it doesn't have any liens on it. Once you give your money over and find this info out later, they may already be long gone. Sometimes on personal issues they remove some things they replaced stock parts with custom radio custom rims. The car might be on some spare rims and tires or stock tires. The radio area may be missing. There is nothing wrong with this, the buyer just wants to sell this separately as it will generate more money for them and leaving it on the car won't raise the value of the car since they will take a low offer just to get the quick cash. To be honest those items may have already been sold and the car was the last option to sell. As always look up the current market value and see what those cars are selling for. It's more than likely that the owner can make more money if they had more time, but time is not on their side, so they'll sell it cheaper just to get the quick cash. It'll be up to you to find out what you want to give them. How much you got to put into it.

Most of the time I am scouring the net looking for parts for vehicles I have or will get soon. I always look at everyone's current sales. I only look at the private car sales. The dealership cars I don't pay attention to. I always want to stay current with my car's market value. I want to know when a model takes a dip, a new model comes out, or when it's time to move on to another year, make and model car. Doing this I always see what others are trying to get for their cars. They are usually asking a lot more than the car is worth and that is good for me because when it's time to sell my car I will stand out every time. Also, this allows me to see if I want to buy someone else's problem. If it's a car I deal with on a daily basis and I have most of the parts that car needs I'll text or call them and see if I can stop by to take a look. Suppose they are offering $5000 for the car and the car is worth 10k in good running condition. The first thing I do is not take $5000, which is what they are asking for. I might bring $4,500 and take out $1,000 and put it somewhere in the car. So, when I do show up, I only have $3,500 on me. Now this is considering the car is in a good location, it's not off the highway or I'm not about to be robbed just to get that out of the way. If the location or people seem sketchy, I call off the deal and turn around. I have no problem turning down a deal and living another day.

Let's say I show up and run through all the checklists I listed previously. While I'm going through this in my head, I'll be asking the buyer some questions to take the focus on what I'm doing and get some general information about the car. Questions like, how long have you had it, how many owners does it have, have you had any problems with it, and if so, what were they? Why are you selling it? If it starts, then I'll want to drive it around the block (and go through those checklists). If it doesn't then it's straight to negotiating. My first question is always the same: so what are you looking to get for it? (knowing I know how much he wants for it). They'll usually come back with their bottom dollar which is lower than the starting price. So now the starting price is lower than where they wanted to start. Then I'll sit back, act like I'm thinking about it and then go over some things I found that will need to be replaced. Then I'll shoot my offer which will be lower than theirs. Not so much that it's disrespectful, but maybe another $500 off. So, if they said they wanted at least $4,500. I'll go over the car and what I saw and offer $4,000. If they say something in between then I'll usually agree with that offer and shake on the deal. If they stay firm on the $4,500 then I'll ask if they can meet me in the middle of $4,000 and $4,500 is $4250. It's only $250 off, but really it's $750 as they initially wanted $5k for it. If they don't agree to that then any offer under $4,500 and I'll jump on the deal. But I will never jump on whatever they put out as their first offer. It's always lower. Then as I say I need to get the money from the car I will ask to see the title first. I need to see the title before any transaction takes place. Once the title has been verified with the VIN on the car then I'll count the money then hand it to the buyer for a second count. After that is done, I'll make sure everything is signed off on the title and I have all the keys for the car. Depending on the situation I may drive the car away right there. I'll leave mine behind as I am the only one who has the keys for it. I don't know if someone else has the keys to the car I just bought and leaving it there is risky. Even if the car breaks down on the way back, I will be the only one who knows where it broke down. If I break down or make it all the way to the house, I'll Uber or Lyft back and get the car I went in first. Make sure you don't roll up in a fancy car with nice wheels. You never know the area you're in even if it's broad daylight.

Once the deal is done, it's time to examine the car and see what's the least amount of work it needs to make sellable as soon as possible. After all, I got a clean title in hand and it already signed over. This is called an open title. When a seller signs It and doesn't put your name directly on it. The state hates it when you do this because it loses tax money on the middleman buyer doing a flip. But hey, it beats waiting around for two weeks for a title to come in and you can sell it much faster. Trust me, no auction is going to leave the title open these days. You will always have to get the title under your name before selling that vehicle. The only way to get an open title these days is to buy it directly from another buyer with the title left blanked and the seller's signature the only one on there (in the appropriate spaces). This is a true quick flip like the old days!

One time a guy was selling a Crown Vic that had a bad miss on it, and he was selling it real cheap. I believe at the time those cars were selling for $5000. All he wanted was $2,000. I showed up and drove it in the parking lot of where he worked. I examined the car and asked what he thought was wrong with it. He said he didn't know (which I knew was a lie) but I just wanted to see his answer. I offered him $1,500 and he said he can do $1,700. I asked for the title, looked it over and gave him 17 one hundred-dollar bills. I drove it home and went back and got my car. Upon the diagnoses I noticed it was something with spark, so I began removing all of the coils and spark plugs. While I was removing one spark plug, I noticed one came out too easy. When I double checked it with another spark plug, I found out the rough idle issue. It was a stripped spark plug in one cylinder (which had been done by the previous owner). I had to purchase a Heli coil kit from the store which was about $10. I rented a Heli coil tool kit with some thread glue and placed it in a new Heli coil. I let it set for 48 hours and then replaced the whole car with new spark plugs (which was about $20). I dove it up and down the highway and it was running great! I took it to the car wash and detailed the inside and outside. Shined the engine bay and shined the tires. Took pictures and listed it. Within 72 hours of purchasing that vehicle I was able to sell it for $5,000.

There have been times where people in my neighborhood ask me to help them sell their vehicle for them and would pay me a fee. I once listed a person's van for $1,200 and saw that van was selling for $4,000 but a mechanic had told them it had a bad transmission. So instead of taking that on as a project I decided to just help them sell it. I posted it for $1,800 and within 6 hours I had 3 people coming to look at it. The first buyer offered me $1,600 and knowing the neighbor only wanted $1,200 for it I jumped on the deal. I made a quick $400 for just taking pictures of it and posting it. I didn't even wash or clean the inside (and they had 4 kids and it was filthy inside). I gave the woman her $1,200 and she gave me $200 for helping her out. Funny thing was the guy who bought it called me the next day and told me he already knew what was wrong with the transmission before he bought it. He said the part was $300 at the dealership and took 2 hours to put it on. He said he sold it to a friend for $4,000 that day. I laughed as it's something I would've done. But I made money while I already had several ongoing projects. Everyone made money so everyone was happy in that situation. Well I say everyone but not the family who asked me to help them sell it. I told them that the buyer fixed what their mechanic told them was going to need a new transmission for $4,000. She was pretty upset that her mechanic told her it was going to be 4k to fix it and it ended up being only $300. I told her the only reason I am telling you this is to always get a second or third opinion on a mechanics work if it seems really high. Her response was paying for a tow truck for $80. You can do the math and I would've paid an extra $160 to save over 3k.

Understanding auctions – online and In-person

Auctions are both online and in person these days. It used to be In-person only even 10 years after the internet was around, shocking right? The benefits of In-person bidding is when there are mistakes with lot numbers, wrong bid amount announced, and re-run of vehicles that stalled or broke down getting into the line. By going to an auction in-person, you get to hear the rearrangements and are notified instantly. Online you sometimes get audio and sometimes you don't. Sometimes the auctioneer is muffled, sometimes they don't even offer audio. Sometimes the online picture is not what is being sold because there was an onsite rearrangement. Sometimes the auctioneer is using a laptop with cheap Wi-Fi and the internet is slow and you get frozen screens. When it comes back on, they have moved through 7 lots. What if one of those lots were the ones you wanted?

Now online does have its own perks too. Let's say there are three or four auctions happening that day and you can't be at all of them in person, but you had your car list lined up and had your backup auction cars if the first ones went too high, what are you going to do if you wanted to be In-person? Here's what you do, if they are local or even if one is local, you go and check them out the day before the auction. Take a clip board, laptop, or use your phone and be prepared to make notes of the vehicles you're interested in. If the auction is In-person, they will most likely not list all the errors or faults the car may have.

They do this on purpose! This way when you buy something you can't complain about something not described as that auction place will ask you, "did you not come and precheck the vehicles?" "Did they not start the vehicle on the day of?" If there is an obvious engine noise and they don't list that in the listing, you are in a losing argument if you won it online and never came and checked it out in person. So, go check out the vehicle(s) if they are local BEFORE you place a bid.

City auctions can be tricky on how they list their cars. I'd say about 90% of the descriptions are from what the fleet manager told the third party auctioneer and what state the vehicle was in before auctioned off. When the auctioneer writes down the lot numbers and takes pictures, they sometimes get a few lot numbers wrong when they get back to the office. When they call and speak to the fleet manager and he forgets too which one had the bad engine or bad transmission it becomes a toss-up come auction day. Both of these people are not losing money on anything, so they'll just make the best guest and mark, whichever the bad transmission or bad engine. Good for the sellers regardless, bad for the buyers. I have been on both sides of this. Once bought a car that was to have 60k miles and ended up having 130k miles. I also bought a car with supposedly engine issues only to find out that the car ran great with no issues.

Another scenario at an auction is when a used car dealer sends in one of his cars that has been on his lot for the past 5 years with 5 previous owners. He's already made 3x more than he paid for it but it's too abused to resale so he sends it to the auction to get whatever he can. The bad is that this seller knows the overdrive is out and runs like crap over 40mph. He knows that an auction won't be able to take it up past 40 mph for the overdrive to kick in. Transmissions are not cheap and fixing that in a car he's already made 3x the amount isn't worth the repair. But he also knows if someone doesn't know about the transmission, they will pay top dollar. So, the scumbag seller sends it to the auction anyways. I have bought these cars and they are mostly from shady dealers. The auctions you go to in-person may split the cars up into groups of known dealers to unknown dealers and this may help you out in identifying such groups. But I've only seen these done at dealer auctions.

Dealer auction prices can go extremely high on the known car dealers like Toyota, Ford, etc. and the lines with unknown dealers most of the cars are passed on with no bids. (Side note: If you are at a public auction and you see a worker you can ask them if that is a dealer car, city car or private seller car. These are valuable tools to use and know). Small dealers are some of the shadiest sellers out there. Crazy thing is they do this to each other not even knowing. Just know there is a risk when buying from a dealer auction. Even known dealers like Chevy and Lexus will (on trade ins) just send in those cars to the auction without even inspecting them. The cars they send to the auction are not even worth the value to put it on their lot. So just because you're buying from a known dealer doesn't make it a 15-point inspection car. All dealers just want to make money, and anything being bought or sold at an auction is like going to Vegas and gambling.

Another downside of online auctions is most places charge an online percentage. It's usually between 2-5% of the final sale price. So not only will you have to pay your local state tax, the 10-15% buyer's premium, the additional admin fee (20-$50), yes you will pay extra because you used their online feature.

Always have a backup plan and a last car in mind option. You never know at these auctions. Sometimes a car you had picked for last place goes sky high in price and a car you thought everyone would want gets passed on and you score a really big! So, check out all the cars beforehand and decide which car is best from top to bottom or the top 10. Don't be afraid to bid early if the price is right! You might just get out of there while the other sharks are fighting over the leftovers

How to bid

Online and in-person bidding are nearly the same. In-person, you've got to wait until the auctioneer goes down to the lowest starting point until someone places a first bid. A typical example is if a car is worth $10,000 and the auctioneer starts off at 10k, you aren't going to bid on it at that price. You wait ... as it goes down to 9k,7k,6k,5k,4k,3k, then someone places a bid, and the bidding begins. Auctioneers hate this as they have to work it all the way back up to 6k and go by $100 increments every time. Some auctioneers would even express their frustration by saying, "C'mon guys, you know the price will still go back up to X amount of dollars, so why do we have to start off at $500 every time." Well, I'll tell you why; it's just because you don't want to jump on $3,000 and be the only one who bids and wins. You'd look around and wonder why isn't no one else bidding on this car? You may have overlooked that car had water in the oil with all the cars you've written down and forgot to add this as a side note of mechanical issues. You would have won the same car for $1500 if you had waited until the auctioneer went to $500 because other people knew about the water in the oil situation, and once you got it, you're not going to be as mad as you were. I mean, I'm always upset, but still go to the lowest bottom dollar and start bidding once the bidding starts.

Sometimes people have an unlimited amount of dollars to win a car and raise their bidding card on everyone who outbids them. Sometimes some dealers want all 3 of a particular model of cars being sold that day and will do whatever it takes to win them all. I've never let those people get away with cheap things and make sure they spend all of their money on the cars they wanted because if I let them off, they may have extra money and buy the cars I want at a very low price. This is only if you are experienced enough to know the bidder you're bidding against because in the end, you don't want to win a car you really never wanted. It's really funny seeing other people doing the same thing to these people. They place their hand over their eyes and eventually raise their bidding card until everyone taps out. Amazing what people will spend just to buy a car. Now, I will give you some bonus material here. Let's assume it's a city selling 10 of the same model cars, and it's only you and another buyer looking at all of them. Do you think it's wise to raise the price and overpay for all of them to help the auctioneers instead of yourself? No, here's what you can do. Ask the other buyer in the middle of the next car being sold (usually a 2-minute delay between cars driving through) and ask them how many they plan on buying. If they say 3 or 5, then ask them how many you want and which ones. Do ensure to work with each other to avoid bidding over each other. Sometimes this works, and sometimes it doesn't. It's called a gentleman's agreement. Now the other buyer could break his agreement after he won his first 5 with no other bidders, and when you go for car 6, he starts to bid against you. You begin to think, "What?" It could be because he got such great deals on his first five and saved over 10k; he has way more money to buy. So, try to make an agreement where you buy one, then he buys one, etc. I can assure you this really works! Sometimes one of you will get unlucky, and even if he doesn't bid on your car, another buyer might decide he wants in, and now you're in competition with this new person. But if the two of you are still in agreement, you can't break the code because you got out-bided on your car. You've got to let it pass on to the other guy. You can do anything you want, but it's best to make friends at these places while you can. If it's an online auction, you run into these buyers a day before the pre-inspection days. You two can make the same agreement for online bidding as you will both know each other's user IDs' name. Online bidding is virtually the same as In Person, only until you wait until the dollar hits rock bottom before you bid. You wait until the last 10 minutes to bid. Here are the reasons why. First, if you are a new bidder to your new auction site, you'd like to wait until the last minute to bid. You actually want to bid right away to see if your bidding number is approved, and you are good to bid on that site. You can select another item on that site to check this if you want. I'd say you pick a really cheap item that you know is worth $1,000 and you place a bid of $100. If you get rejected or denied, contact the auction place immediately to find out what's wrong with your bidder number. You might have to place a certain amount of deposit. I've been to auctions where $500 gets you a certain bidding card where $1,000 gets you an all-access bidding card. So, make sure you are good to bid before you wait until the last minute.

When it comes time to bid, you may realize the bidding is either A much higher or B hasn't moved at all in the past few days. If it's too high, just watch it for fun and don't get into a bidding war due to your ego. Always have the highest amount you'd pay for a car and leave it at that. Find out what's the most you can make on that car, and there is no higher dollar you'd pay.

So, it's within the last 10 minutes and let's say the car you're looking at is selling for 10k on the market, and it's been at $1,500 for the past few days. Now within the last 10 minutes, it goes up and is now at 3k. Assuming you have a set price at 5k. The auction is within the last 5 minutes and there is no extension bidding (extended bidding kicks in when someone bids within the last 5 minutes. It puts it back to 5 minutes every time someone does this. It will keep going on until someone finally taps out). Be sure to put your final bid within the last 5-15 seconds of the auction ending. Most bidders will snipe a bid at the last second, but if your bid is way higher, then you win! I have been in bidding wars with someone for over an hour, going back and forth with $20 increments each time with bid extensions. You just have to wait for it sometimes, although it depends on what you're bidding on and how badly you want it. Now there is another feature where there is no extended bidding, whereby it ends when the bidding ends. Much like eBay, there is no extended bidding. When there is no extended bidding, it's where the price can go crazy within the last few seconds. So be prepared to put in your highest bid within the last 5 seconds if you have an extremely high internet speed. Ensure you are not on your phone or there is no one in your house using up all the internet speed. If you have kids and everyone is streaming or playing games, you might have to be the person who bids within the last

10 seconds instead of the last few seconds. eBay is good because it gives you the second countdown and has a really good internet speed. When you have these moms and pops auctions and everyone slams their hosted servers, it can cause a bottleneck and the bidding freezes for 10 seconds until it refreshes. You don't want to be the person who entered $4,999 on a 5k limit, whereas the item sells for $3500. Bid early if you have slow internet speed; bid last if you're gutsy and a risk-taker! Benefits could pay off, or you could be mad for the next few hours wishing you had more time. The choice is yours!!

Where to sell

Prices! Prices! Prices! This is the topic for today. There are so many options to choose from in this field. But you have to know what you're selling and what kind of price you're looking for to determine what platform to sell it on. There is nothing for free these days. Every site wants you to either pay for an individual sale, or they want you to pay a subscription, or they want to take a profit off the sale or even sometimes both!

I am going to go through a few that I use, and you can determine which ones to try. Again, you have to know your vehicle because you can lose money posting on a site wanting a fee upfront for an X amount of days and you get nothing but wasted time and money

So, let's start with eBay. eBay you can choose from a couple of options. It all about the days you want to have it posted is where the fees kick in. For example, you can choose 7 days and pay $50 to post your car or you can post for 30 days for $100. You can choose 3 days, but I really don't know who ever uses that. I mean why would you pay anything for your car to be only posted for 3 days. The longer you have it on eBay's site the more views you will get. Now for the tricky parts. You have the option to use an auction format (which will require bids) or you can choose a fixed sale which you are able to post your starting point and the only bid required will end up winning the vehicle. But this comes with so many stipulations. First, now this is very important! You want to make sure you check the check box that an immediate deposit is required to purchase this vehicle. If you do not check this box in the fixed format anyone that just joined can win your car without a deposit and if they do not pay (which most new users don't even understand the concepts of buying a vehicle on eBay) you will lose your $100 listing fee. Because in eBay's eyes you sold your car. Now in some cases you can call eBay to disclaim the seller etc. and they may give you your money back, but this may be a one and only time for your ever existence on eBay. So, take it from me, check this check box! Also, on the fixed rate it is a good idea to check the box to Allow buyers to make an offer. You have the option to set a lowest dollar amount you are willing to take, or even the highest dollar amount that someone can offer and automatically win once they hit the correct numbers. Personally, I never set a highest dollar amount. I set the starting point amount and I set the lowest I'm willing to take for the vehicle. With the process you can see which users are offering lowball offers etc. and you will not be notified of that offer. If you don't set a lowest offer you will get every offer out there even if someone is offering $100 for your car. So, to eliminate the lowball offers just set the lowest you're willing to take. If you don't end up selling your car for your starting price or even your lowest offer, you get the option to send an offer to someone who made an offer below the lowest price you set. I don't get any sales this way as most buyers will look at the sale like you overpriced the vehicle and they may offer you even a lower price, but that option is always there if you're willing to go that route. Bargaining with buyers is key when you set your lowest price. Depending on your sale you can risk it by going back and forth with a buyer on the price using eBay's counteroffer feature. But it is risky! You can lose a buyer if you go too high. They may either let the offer expire or simply decline your offer. So again, it is up to you to determine your negotiating price. I usually go about $500 as a counteroffer to see how much they are interested in that car. If they don't counteroffer, they really weren't that serious. Remember a buyer can counteroffer with the same price they initially offered without raising a penny. Now here is an important piece to remember. If you and the buyer agree to a set price your auction will automatically be sold to that person and removed from eBay (WITHOUT that person having to submit the deposit you required) Counteroffers dismisses the deposit requirements. But you are able to see the buyer's feedback and determine if you're willing to give up that option. I usually send a message directly to the buyer and tell them to text or call me to consider their offer (regardless of their feedback). If I don't hear anything I don't even move forward with their offer. With serious buyers I usually get a call, we talk about the vehicle and come up with a price on the phone so then I can send them the agreed upon offer. I never just send an offer without a text or phone confirmation before sending an offer.

eBay's auction price is a bit different. There are no offers. You only have the option at a starting price and a reserve price (if you're willing to pay the extra reserve fees). There is no deposit requirement. Anyone is able to bid even if they just joined (there is a feature to block people with negative feedback, but it's really useless as it's the new members who are the risky ones to begin with). So, this is a big gamble! You have options to hide bidder's information but usually this comes off as you may be bidding on your own vehicles. Because on eBay if you are a good seller you will have followers and those followers will keep an eye on who bids and who wins on your vehicles. So, I strongly disagree with hiding buyers' bidding ID. eBay does its own block info on bidders' info but it can still show feedback numbers and buyers are smart enough to read between the lines and see if you are using shill bidders to bid on your own vehicles. So, keep it straight and keep your sales honest and buyers will respect you and your sales. Plus, it's easier to sleep at night.

On your description on eBay make sure you post everything you require from your payments, to pick up, to warranty. Buyers will use things against you if you don't put your requirements. This is key and without these requirements buyers can use the smallest things you didn't post to cancel on the whole deal and again you are out of listing fees and time. I post on all my sales what payment options I require, how long until they have to make payment, how long I can hold the vehicle after payment is received, how the buyer needs to setup pickup and or vehicle transportation, and last is to inspect the vehicle and ask all questions before placing a bid and there is no warranty on the vehicle I am selling. The warranty may change depending on that vehicle. I place my number on the ad and wish everyone well and happy bidding

Now I am going to consume Offer up, Autotrader, CarGurus, Craigslist all together. All of these sites require different settings, but all in all they are not auction sites, so they all tend to sell the same cars but with different prices. Offer up offers 3 listings for free each month and $5 each listing after that until the month expires then it resets. You have the option to promote your listing for $20 per month to put your vehicle at the top of the list, but you can only do this to one of your sales. Personally, I have great success with the promote feature and $20 per month helps me sell things quicker and after I sell that one item, I move it to the next available item I want to sell the quickest. Craigslist is $5 to list a vehicle. There are no promotions or anything else to help boost your listing. You have a max of 10 auto listings until you can no longer list anymore. Each time you list if sets your car at the top of the list. So, if you only have one car for sale you can keep listing it every day (or every 2 days is what I do) to keep putting it at the top so it can generate more views. Craigslist works a lot like google or any similar search engine. After about 3 or 4 pages you seem to tune out on cars. A person can narrow down their search on craigslist (if they are experienced with the site) to see fewer results. But if they just type in Ford Taurus, they will see every year and every part and car people are selling on Craigslist. It really muddies the waters. Cars are the only thing that Craigslist makes you pay $5 for. Some people post in car parts the car they are selling just to list it for free, but they can go unnoticed if a user just narrows down their search. So, don't be cheap and just pay the $5 to list your vehicle where it belongs. As long as you have your car set a few bucks below everyone else you will get clicks and calls on your vehicle. Applying the two-day method to help boost your car I have found it very useful and usually sell a car within 2 weeks of having the car for sale on Craigslist

CarGurus and Autotrader and pretty much the same sites owned by different companies. The philosophies are the same. You post for the vehicle for 30 days and have the ability to renew the listing. It's a little bit more sophisticated than craigslist like people have the ability to set a schedule to view the vehicle, send private messages, and even allow buyers to determine the value of the vehicle using their platform's car value blue book feature. Now they may not be correct, but it still generates the basic value of your vehicle for sale. In CarGurus using the car values feature against it determines if your car is considered an average deal, good deal, or great deal. If you can land your car in the great deal section your car will be automatically promoted on the top of the listings thus getting more views. I don't like using CarGurus because it always values my car lower than what the market values is and I would have to list it at a ridiculous price—lower than what I paid for it to be considered a great deal. I have tried CarGurus several times and I have had no success. Although I have a friend who uses it all the time and has great success selling cars, the profits are really not worth it. The good thing about Autotrader and CarGurus is it promotes your cars on a vastly wider scale to the smallest auctions, car selling sites etc. but if you don't fall into the great deal categories your car really doesn't reach the people who are looking for your kind of deals. I find these two sites are best for selling finance vehicles. These are not really built for flipping cars for quick cash. You want to make money in finance charges and payments then these are the sites to go to.

Facebook marketplace is another trending source that is also free. It's pretty simple where you post some pics and list a small description. People will then message you through Facebook's Messenger app. Side note: because it's Facebook, don't think that shady people don't try to sell on there. I was interested in a jet ski, but the seller wanted to sell it without a title. However, he said he could get a title.

How to make the best listings and sell

Most online used car selling websites now have the option to do everything from your iPhone or android. But there are some phone apps that are only phone accessible only (or you can only post pictures from your phone but can still access messages through your computer).

Offer Up, Craigslist, Autotrader, 5 miles, CarGurus are some of the more popular ones to use.

Here are some key features when listing:

1. Make sure you clean your car BEFORE you post any pictures of your car. That will be the interior, exterior and engine compartment. Throw away old water bottles, trash, combs, CD's or whatever you have lying around to distract the buyer from any potential misunderstandings
2. Make sure there is daylight available. Don't take pictures with a flash in your garage
3. Take a picture of the car in a whole at different angles. Don't cut off your images with the part of the front end missing. Walk around the vehicle taking many pictures, I'd say about 30-40, you can always delete later but you'd have to retake more just to get better shots if you missed any
4. Try to get a good background for your pictures. Anything is better than your apartment in the background or your house that has other broken-down cars sitting around. I prefer the back of a store, a warehouse, a park, an empty parking lot,

you get the picture. You don't need to post your car in a fancy neighborhood with a mansion in the background.

5. Make sure you either remove your license plate or black it out in editing before you upload your photos to a website/ phone app. The thing is some people can look up your license info and show up to your house or possibly steal something. You just never know and if buyers ask you why just tell them by state laws you cannot transfer license plates, that is up to the buyer at their local tax state office (Tax Title and License). You are just following state and local guidelines. I have sold people cars with license plates only to receive a run red light in another state mailed to my home address. Then having to contest that ticket through a lengthy process only because I'd thought I'd help that person get back home safely. I would look into your state tax title website and see if they offer a 72 hr. or 30-day paper plate so a buyer can get home legally and without your name on it. Some states even allow to submit the VIN and a sold notice to update the state the car is no longer in your possession

6. Shine the tires and engine compartment! It's best to go to the local car wash and with $5 clean the exterior and interior of the car. If the fuse box and the wires under the hood are protected, I would throw little suds in the engine bay to clean up any dirt or oil in there. Don't go heavy in there as water can get into the electrical compartment or seep into the ignition coils and either make the car not

start or run rough after starting up. Then you're buying new ignition coils and letting the water dry out before you leave. After your car is dried off, shine the rubber on the wheels with some sort of tire shine. They will make a big difference when taking a picture later in the sun. Also get some engine cleaner or shine and spray all of the black rubber pieces. Then get a rag and wipe off the run-off. If you don't it's possible the shine will wear off with the heat from the motor and it will look similar to before. A small rag and a little cleaning go a long way. I've had buyers ask me why my engine compartment looked so dirty compared to other vehicles in the pictures. I thought, "How would that make a difference when there is nothing wrong with the engine or car's performance?" But every little thing matters and will determine who wants to come out and see your car in person.

7. Choosing a title. Keep it simple. Put in the year make and model and some key features like LOW MILES, or CLEAN TITLE, or V8 or 4x4. All of these things are major differences that will separate your car from the others. Maybe everyone else is asking the same price you're asking for but it's a 2WD two-wheel drive and you have a 4x4 or All Wheel Drive AWD.

8. Listing the description: Again, point out all of the main title features one again. Then you add all of the sub features your car has like Navigation, Cold A/C, Standard or Automatic, all electronics are in good working condition, or New Paint, New motor with warranty.

9. Don't put everything you've done to the car mechanically. I know you want to be an honest seller but doing so will maker buyers question the car rather than your honesty. Trust me, car salesmen have ruined it for everybody. Now buyers will look past the things you list because it sounds like you're coming off desperate or there's major problems with your car. If you put a new starter, spark plugs, alternator, battery, fuel pump, ignition coils, fuel injectors etc. someone will think your car has major starting problems and you threw everything at it just to sell it. If it runs and drives and starts up every time, then that's all the buyer needs to know to help them keep peace in their mind they aren't buying a lemon. Now I have flat out told people there is something wrong with the transmission etc. if it's noticeable and I don't have the funds or time to fix it and would rather sell it as is. Those times I will list the issues in the ad. The price will be cheap. And it will be an extremely hard sell to anyone with a brain. I've sold them but mainly to mechanics. I have also been truthful about everything I've changed, and people just look at me like I'm lying anyways and trying to make a sale. If I've changed the motor and have receipts/warranty to back it up, then yes, I will post it. But if I had the motor rebuilt really cheap and it came with no warranty, but it was running great, then I'd list it as is and not mention anything. Because only mentioning it is only going to raise warranty questions and you will be sitting on that car for a long time until you remove that part and

relist your car 30 days later. Trust me when I say this, if your car has over 150k miles and you had the motor rebuilt and you put on the ad rebuilt motor, I'd say about 90% of the people who run across your ad will think you are lying about the rebuild just to get rid of the car. Go back to the used car salesmen ruining it for everyone.

10. Do not lie in your ad. I can't tell you how many times I've had people text me, call me or show up in person and tell me the horror stories about what a previous seller listed only to find out it was much worse in person. If someone isn't buying my car it isn't because I lied about the title status, the deployed airbags, the car pulling to the right when driving or a brake or turn signal doesn't work, it's because the buyer came and wanted a better car in better condition. I sell used cars not new. There will always be something off here or there mainly because it's not new. Some people really want a new car for a used car price and that just isn't happening. You can't get discouraged about this. It's all a part of the used car selling business. I sell cars that are selling for $25k at the lot for 12k but only because it has a cloth interior or doesn't have the navigation or sunroof. When buyers show up, they point out these things in disappointment and I just remind them of the price. They usually agree with me and say I thought it was going to be better. Sure, and I'm not asking for the better price. Do not let this get to you. They are not putting your car down; they just wanted something not realistic. The people who are shopping and know the difference

in the features and title status, know when they are getting a good deal. Those are the buyers who you're looking for. You can't sell a used car to someone who wants a car fully loaded for an unreasonable price. Sometimes people think someone is going through a bad marriage or there was a death in the family and that was the deceased person's car. Again, it's wishful thinking and you just move on to the next potential buyer.

11. Key things to list: your description, your phone number, and your price. I don't list my email or respond to emails. Usually those are scammers looking to send you a fraud check and paying extra for the shipping charge. Hoping your bank is dumb enough to give you a false deposit and they get a free car

12. Where to meet: This depends on your schedule. You can take your car to work and sell it during your lunch break. Or you can meet at a local grocery store or park. You can send them your home address but remember they can show up at your doorstep at any given time unannounced. You can meet at a police station but wherever you meet just make sure it's in a well crowded area. Also make sure you are close to a highway in case the buyer wants to see how it handles above 50 mph. Never let a buyer get up to a 100 mph. I've had this happen and the police were ready to take that person to jail. It only takes 60 mph for the OD or overdrive to kick in and to properly go through all the gears in the transmission. And if there were problems in the steering, braking system and

cooling system things would be noticeable at those speeds and the engine idling for over 10 minutes. Make sure the driver has a driver license. You may have to explain some of these things to a buyer because without it you give them authorization with your silence and just seeing those dollar signs

13. Bonus: This is more of proper test-driving procedures than how to list, but I'd figure I'd put this in here. Insurance is a big deal. If you cannot afford it, you have to be very careful whoever you let test drive your car. Never let someone just take the keys and drive off without you being inside the vehicle. I don't care if they brought a whole family, one of them is staying behind so you can ride inside. No joking I've had people take off for over an hour test driving and them not answering their phone. Only for them to come back and say they got lost

Dealing with in person customers vs online customers

Let's first talk about dealing with people face to face. This is where you'll generate most if not all of your sales! The best thing you can have in your favor, is to have one of the best cars in your market for sale. Have it set at an unbeatable price and have it looking super clean that even you are impressed with it every time you see it. Each and every person that comes and looks at your car will first judge the neighborhood you live in, the clothes you wear, and then the car. I think people would second guess if you're selling a one-year old corvette at a really low price while living in a poor neighborhood. I have had people ask me if I had a gun on me while we were taking a test drive to see if they were going to get robbed. So, know the basics first. I'm not saying you can't sell in a poor neighborhood; I'm just trying to put you in the buyer's shoes and see where they're coming from first. Heck, I've had people drive by my car for sale and not even get out to look at it and just drive off. Then text me and tell me it's not what they're looking for. I sell my cars what I think the value is. It's never higher because it's always lower, but it's only lower because it's not the higher end model. Some people don't know the differences and come to find out it's not what they had in mind and don't even want to get out and look at it. Hey, it's better than someone not interested and getting me out there to go over the car and waste just a huge amount of time for nothing. Believe me, some people will do this anyhow. They will tell the other person they came with (usually the person interested in the car) to go ahead and take a test drive. Even though it's not the car they are looking for. They just want to get a feel for that model car to see if they even want to go look at the more expensive one. That pisses me off. They know that if they went to a dealership to do this, that dealership will make them stay there for a while, get a copy of their driver license, run their credit report, all before they take a test drive. It could literally take about 1.5 hours just to take a test drive. So, it's sad but some people will take advantage of your situation.

Alright so you got your clothes right, you're groomed, you're doing your best to look the most presentable and show you're a non-threat (again funny, but you have to edge out all sketchiness if possible) and you walk up to the customer. Most likely they will reach out to shake your hand if they are in a good mood. If they don't, then you know they are questionable about the car in front of them. They are not sold on it and they might be thinking something you'll never know about. Now you can try to pick their brain and ask (as if you were an employee at a dealership), what questions do you have, or so what do you think? I say this is a horrible idea. Look if they don't like it, so what, someone else will. The car usually sells itself. It's a used car. They are not at a known dealership and yes not all used cars are going to be as if they were new. When I run into these types of situations, I usually just stand there and keep quiet. The customers will go through the usual checking of the interior, engine oil, starting up the vehicle. Sometimes they will come to the conclusion they are overthinking the situation and come to terms they are in front of a good car with a good deal. If not, they won't be there more than 5 minutes and will thank you for their time. Don't let this get you down. Selling used cars is a numbers game. You are not going to sell everyone a car like it was a new car. You have to walk away knowing you have a good car you're selling and that the right buyer will come along and buy your vehicle. You just have to be patient. This can be tough if your first five customers in person have all walked away. Now, don't keep walking away not gaining anything from what the previous buyers have whispered or made comments to a friend or relative they brought with them about your car. If they mention certain things like, "Oh, it's missing the molding here," "the paint is peeling," or "the seats are too dirty," you'll have to consider getting things cleaned, replacing parts you thought would go unnoticed, or even getting the car painted. You'll have to consider you might lose $300 but you'll still make money off the deal. It can get depressing when you're hitting around the eight mark of people not interested in your vehicle. You're going to have to either consider lowering the price a whole lot and then bring up the low price when someone mentions the paint, or you might have to drop in extra money in paint just to move the sale.

The art of staying silent: One of your biggest selling points is to listen rather than blab about how good your car is. When you are a salesmen on a car dealer lot you have hundreds of new cars to choose from so you can keep talking until you figure out what the person is looking for (if they haven't had a car in mind already) Believe me, so many people walk into a new car place with one car in mind and a good salesmen will end up selling them something different just because it makes the company and that salesman more money. So, stay silent about your car for sale unless the person asks specific questions. You'll want to do the basics and say hello, shake a hand or two (considering viruses, heh) and just stand back and let the people inspect the car. Most of the time they'll have one or more people with them to validate their suspicions or questions they have. Even if you overhear their conversations and you know they are getting or giving wrong advice to each other, don't jump in and cut them off. Stay silent and see if it's a car they are interested in. Here's the thing, people know what they are looking for when it comes to a used car. The same rules that apply to a new car dealership as mentioned does not apply to used cars. They may have been looking for used cars for the past month. They may have already seen about 20 or more cars just like yours. Trying to correct them, prove them wrong, etc. is not going to win anything in your favor. If they don't want it, you won't be able to convince them otherwise. You can try to experiment and try to win the battles just for giggles but know that you already lost the sale and you can try to save it if you want. Will you be successful? Possibly not, but you may get some laughs for your humor, or yawl both may leave this situation in an argument with both of yawl leaving without saying goodbye. Now if they ask you what's the history, or what can you tell me about it, then yes, they are asking for your advice on the situation. If they ask what size the engine is and how long you have had it, answer them. Just don't' start offering these things when there is silence. Offering these things is only going to make it feel like a pressure to the buyer. Have you ever been to a clothing store where a person walks up to you and asks you if you need anything when you just got there? You're like, I just got here can I look first, thank you. Although you may not say those exact words, it's the same thing when it comes to car shopping. Let the buyers look, let them talk amongst each other, and if they ask questions answer them. The question you want is what's the least you'll take is what you really want.

Ok, let's say you get past the initial car condition—now comes the money part. Not a whole lot of people are just going to pay your asking price without some negotiating. Only once did I have a person just hand over the amount I was asking for. As awesome as it would seem to get everything you asked for, once I counted the money, I handed the gentleman back $200 and told him, you need to negotiate the price on everything. He was young and I hope I gave him a lesson. The buyer will ask the question, so what are you asking for it again? Knowing they know the price they want to see where the starting point is. I usually respond, "It's listed at [X amount of dollars]" and then stay quiet. I never negotiate my own price. They drove out to my place and they already know where the starting price is, but it's the game you have to play. Also, why would you negotiate your own price if you shoot under what the buyer had in mind. So just stand there and wait for the buyer to respond. They may come off a couple of hundred bucks and then you can make a deal. Or they might try to lowball you and go about $2,000 under. You can't sit there and think about the price if you feel it is a disrespectful offer. If you've done your research, and you know the market value of your car vs what other people are selling theirs you should know when someone is low balling your price knowing nobody else is even selling close to what they are offering. You might call them out on it, and they might say they have another car they're looking at if they don't buy yours. I wouldn't ask to see this other car because they won't be able to find it anyways because it's made up, I just respond with, well that sounds like a deal I'm not going to be able to match. You can then offer your bottom deal and if they try to go $500 under your bottom deal then that's up to you to decide how much you're making and how much you've invested into your car. You already know no one is selling it at the price they're asking to pay you for yours, so usually I just stick to my lowest price. Now if they do some hard negotiating, I'll go another $100 off my lowest price just to show them they are winning the deal. Again, it all depends on how long you've had your car listed and how many people have turned away on your car. If you've only had it listed for 2 days and someone is trying to offer you this insane low price, I will usually pass. I've had people show me all the cash they had in front of me asking if I'm sure I won't sell it to them and I'll just tell them I'm good and good luck finding a car that cheap. I've had a guy do this to me and within an hour I sold it to the next guy with $500 of my asking price when the first guy wanted $1,500 off. You have to know when to walk a deal on a person because you've done your homework and you're not going to just give a deal away because someone else knows how to play hardball with you. There's something when you see your own car reposted from the guy you just sold it to for a higher price than you had it and knowing they just bought it from you to flip and make a profit from your hard work.

The last thing is, invest in a counterfeit dollar pen marker. There are not many people out there using fake money to buy things, but I've heard stories, and I encountered it once when I was selling a set of wheels I had for sale. Some guys pulled up without out of state plates, wanted me to help them load the wheels in the car to see if they would fit, then before they left, they handed me two, one hundred dollar bills. They looked smaller than the regular ones. Then as I looked closer, I saw the numbers on the bills were the same. So, people do try and pass fake bills out there. Had it been a car deal I would've caught on sooner and wouldn't have marked all the bills with the counterfeit pen. Also, try not to do business in an unknown place after dark. Now I have sold several cars after 8pm, it was always sketchy with me being alone and the other person having two people. Now it's usually the opposite where the person robbing is the person selling but you just never know, and I'd hate to say do this without caution. We've all heard stories so use your best judgment when it comes to night sales

Online Customers:

These will be done though well organizations like eBay, CarGurus, Autotrader, etc. These places make a profit off the sale or make profits off the listing fees etc. But online customers can be some of these best people to deal with. Why? Because once they win the car, they will either text you for your bank info or they will ask for your number to get this same info. They will pay the deposit fee if you have one, or they will pay for the vehicle with a credit card, bank cashier's check, or wire transfer and you'll get your money instantly. The one thing you have to do is to be honest in your listing. It's crazy because you might miss a thing and that one thing could give you a bad seller rating on one of those trusted sites. I've had a guy give me bad feedback because not all the bolts were bolted down in the back seats and he had to go buy 4 nuts from the dealer that cost $5 a piece and he was upset I didn't put that in the listing. Heck I didn't even see that due to the seats working just fine. So even though you'll get your money instantly, be sure to describe your vehicle as best as you can. I always put a disclaimer in my ads that I have listed everything to the best of my knowledge and anything not seen or listed cannot be held at the seller's response. I know it sounds bland and covers a whole grey area but again I don't want to get blamed for something I didn't list. Not intentionally but maybe a switch didn't work, or a knob.

After you have set up the money transfer and you now have it in your bank account, you then work with the buyer to set up a time when they plan on picking up the vehicle. They should either be traveling by plane or will set up a shipping transport company to pick up the vehicle. If they have questions about auto transport companies be sure to check this out for yourself and get familiar with how auto transport companies work. Most are brokers who take a deposit and set up a driver to pick up a vehicle on their behalf. You don't want to be clueless in this situation. You don't want to lose potential buyers if they mention they are new to the site and don't want to travel by plane but are unsure about auto transport. You don't want to tell them you've never dealt with that and to go find that info out themselves. That might be too much for a person and they may turn down the whole situation over the auto transport. So, set up how they plan on picking up the vehicle and set a date when they expect to pick up the car. Just because you have the money the car is still in your possession and you are still liable to it if anything happens. It gets damaged by weather or is stolen. I always put a two-week limit. I can hold the vehicle and put a date on it. You can determine your own schedule but without one some people might just wait up to a month on a trip they had planned 30 days out. If nothing is ever said, the date is really open

Scheduling people to come see your car

If we lived in a perfect world where things came easy a buyer would say they are on their way and will be seeing you in a little bit. But sadly, this is always an uncharted territory. Yes, you have to take every call or text seriously and have to set up a schedule. If you don't set a schedule and you happen to give a person your address, then it is possible that person may show up at any time since you both never mentioned a specific time. I will always set a date and time and then tell that person to be sure to text or call me before they come out, and to never just show up. I have had people show up hours later only to find out I'm not even home nor is the car as I was driving it at the time. If I have a hot car that is getting multiple texts and calls within the hour and people want to come see that car, I don't just give out my address and tell everyone the first person with cash that shows up buys it. I've done this and it was never good.

The problem with setting times to close is people are usually late to arrive and then you'll have the first person show up 10 minutes before the second person was to show and now you have one buyer sitting in the background waiting to see if the first person decides to buy it or not. You might be thinking okay I have a backup if the first person doesn't want it, but no that isn't what that buyer is thinking. You as the seller hope you sell it to the first person and have to tell the second person, "Sorry, but the car is now sold." Trust me, you really do want to sell it to the first person who offers you a cash deal. Don't expect to turn down the first deal if it's lower than you wanted in hopes of selling it to higher to the second person. Here's what will happen. The second person will see the first person didn't want it for whatever reason. They won't know if you were haggling over an offer or if the buyer just didn't want it. The only thing they see is the first person driving away going to possibly look at another vehicle. This is never good and usually ends up with both buyers leaving without your car. The second person will think the other buyer saw something they couldn't see and they don't want to be the person who buys something only to find out it's a costly repair and they just bought a money pit car. I would say almost 100% of situations I have been in similar to this I was unfortunate to sell to anyone. Now if you're thinking, what about the first person's offer, can you call them back. The problem with that is if they get a call from you it means that the second person didn't want it and now you are their only hope. So, they will either refuse your offer or offer you even a lower price to the first agreed price. You'll end up walking that person. Now if the second person offers you even a lower price than the first person you can smile and tell them the first person offered you more but you had to turn them down because you can get more for your car. Then the second person will say, "Yeah but I'm the only one here, so do you want to sell it to me for this low price or what?" You'll end up walking that person too.

I've had a situation where a first buyer showed up late and then the second buyer showed up immediately after we had just test drove the car. So, the first buyer told me to go ahead and help the people who just showed up while he thought about the price. So, I agreed and began to talk with the second set of people. During that conversation the first buyer said he had to talk to me and when I went to talk with him, he gave me an offer and a written check in the amount he wanted to pay for the car. The price was fair and just as I was about to sell the car the second people (it was a man and women) the woman told the husband that he should test drive the car real quick just to see if it's the car he's looking for because she knew it was about to be sold to the other buyer. So instead of telling them I just sold the car I gave the guy my keys and told him he can drive it around the block really quick. The guy took the keys and drove it around the block. In that short time the first guy said he was going to wait in his truck until the second guy came back. He went to his truck, sat there for about a minute then started up the truck and drove off. I thought he might've just gone to the store for a quick drink, or my second thought was he just realized he wanted to keep looking to see what else is out there. When the second guy showed back up, he gave me the keys and just looked at the vehicle. I looked at the wife and said, "Well I hope your husband wants it because I just lost a paying buyer to let you drive the vehicle". The woman asked if he wanted it and of course, he said he wanted to keep looking. Boy was I frustrated! I knew right then and there that buyers really don't care who's first and who's serious about buying it. They really don't care if the first person had bought it. They might seem like they cared, but who cares about someone's feelings, we aren't here to make friends. We are here to make money.

When two people arrive at the same time and the second person waits, they are always examining the situation. It never ends well. During that process the second person has so much power if the first person doesn't buy. So, you better try and sell the hell out of the car or make sure the first person doesn't want it before moving on to the next buyer. Even if the first buyer wants to put a deposit on it just to make the other person out of the question, I say no to that too. Unless it's a $1,000 deposit, I would say the car is sold to the next guy/ girl. But if they offer $500 or something small, I would pass and just tell them to contact you when they get all the money. Because I would take the risk that the second person has all the money or will offer me a better deal. $500 can always be requested back from the first person. You'd have to write up a receipt etc. so it's not like you can just keep that money (unless you put that the deposit is nonrefundable), but I think that buyer wouldn't agree to that. $1,000 is on the side that the person is serious enough to come and pay the rest. They might not come back the very next day like they said they would but within 2 or 3 days they'll contact you on setting up a time to pay the rest and pick it up from you.

My rule of thumb is to set an hour and a half for each buyer to come and take a look at the vehicle. I give the extra 30 min for the traffic. Then I give another 30 min for them to look it over and test drive it. Then I give the last 30 min to clean up, remove etc. what the first person said was an issue to them from buying it (overhearing chatter as previously mentioned in other chapters). But if the first person showed up at the same time the second buyer showed up, then I would talk to the second buyer first and tell the first buyer you had another person scheduled at a later time and now you are just following your scheduling. If they leave over that then fine. I'm not going to make the second person wait for an extra 30 min extra, or even 5 min for the first person to just look at it, start it up and say they don't want it. I don't want to give that benefit to the first person to possibly ruin it for the second buyer. You can do whatever you want, but based on my experience, I suggest that you do not put in favors to anyone you've never met before. This is your business and you are following your business standards. What's a good responsible business without setting your own standards?

Schedule, set a time and place, and prepare for no shows and flaky people. I can't tell you how many times I have texted with people a day before and they swear up and down they will be there the next day or morning and not to sell the car. Then the day when you never hear from them again. It would be pointless to text or call them because you'll just get a BS answer or no answer at all. I've had people say they were in town and something came up but will be back the next day. The BS stories are countless. But in the business expect this will happen on every sale. There will always be timewasters, window shoppers or people who just want to come and test drive your car because they always wanted to drive your make and model without going to the dealership and spend an hour or so with an employee just to drive one of their dream cars. Who better than to call a private seller and show up, drive their car and walk away within 10 min of conversation? It's impossible to know other people's motives, but you have to give them reason of doubt in case they are serious.

How to respond to texts

I'm going to be upfront with you on this: texting and window shoppers are usually time wasters. In rare cases I have had people ask what my bottom dollar was, and they showed up with the money and bought the vehicle. But that is rare. How rare? Like maybe once in a year. Usually, people who text and ask about the car's condition are people who are about to come into money and are just checking their options. They may even schedule a time to meet up, drive the car and will tell you, "well I'm just waiting on my check, my tax refund, my insurance check etc. and I'll call you later if you still have it." You might think this is good and you're getting some traction on your car. Well, it's not. Unless you like getting your time wasted, you need to ask them the same questions they ask you. If they tell you they are waiting for a payment and don't have all the money yet, you need to tell them to call or text you when you do have the money before you come out. They might get angry with you but it's not worth the trouble. I know you won't listen to me and think you got to try every option out there, like don't ignore the poorly dressed guy in the store because most rich people don't like to show their wealth in public etc., but you will find out these people are only window shopping and will end up wasting your time. Here's what happens on their end. They call all of these people and line up a bunch of cars to look at. They give the same speech to everyone they talk to. They go out and test drive each year's makes and models. In the end, when they are still waiting for their check to come in, they continue to keep looking and more cars become of interest than yours. When and if they finally get their check you never hear from them, and you realize it was all for nothing. And never call a person back after two weeks have gone by to see if they ever got their check etc., because you are letting that person know you haven't gotten any sales or any potential buyers looking at your car and you are just lowering the value of your asking price. Working as an employee at a known dealership is a totally different thing. Those people have to make outgoing calls on walk in customers. Those people have to meet a certain gross profit in order to hit their sales. Those people have no investment in any cars they sell on that lot. You are a different entity but still in the same field. My advice is that anyone who comes to see your car in-person after they send you a text and they walk or tell you, "I'll let you know," just leave it at that. Don't ever follow up on those people.

Another thing you'll often get is: "What's your lowest price?" This is another time waster. What you'll do is give them some random number and they'll reply back with a lower price than what you offered what your lowest price is. Do you not see the disappointment already? They are just throwing numbers around. You can give them a good bottom dollar just for giggles and they still won't show up. What's-the bottom-dollar-people via text are just time wasters. Those people have a set dollar amount and want to see if you are willing to sell your car for whatever they have. I have had people tell me they only have $3,000 on a car I'm selling for $6,000 and my lowest is $5,000. But they will keep texting me asking if I would sell it to them for

$3,000 and they are being serious. It's comical if anything and I usually tell them to go to a fast-food place and order a $10 meal and tell them you only have $5.

Lowballers: I wrote a chapter on this "How to buy a used car for a flip" with people selling their cars and sometimes you can have good success, but it can be time consuming. Lowballers are usually other used car dealerships preying on those who are in need of fast cash and are unable to do a payday loan with their car because they have bad credit etc. They will shoot prices that are ridicules, flat out stupid and can rather be insulting. When you call them out on how stupid their offer is, they usually reply with, "well it doesn't hurt to ask, or it just an offer you don't have to be rude." Yes, you can be rude when someone is offering an 80% discount on the car you're selling. Try going to a real-estate seller and tell them you'll pay 10k for a 100k house. They'll just look at you and laugh. The sad thing is there are people who are hurting, and any type of money is better than no money and some people will sell their cars cheap depending on their situation. I will never go that low when I am in the reverse position, but lowballers are just people throwing out a fishing line to see who will bite. They will do this to about 100 sellers a day. They know who's new and who's not new to whatever site you are on. I have spoken to these people and some of the deals they've come across are amazing! I've heard of one guy getting a 10k Benz for a 1,000 only because the wife didn't want to keep seeing the dead husband's car every day in the garage and she just wanted it gone. Like I said these people will throw many lines out a day, and it's usually a bust. These types of deals are only once in a blue moon or once in a year types of bargains. I strongly disagree with lowballing other sellers as this is not the true art of car flipping to my standards. I usually don't reply to lowball offers and if I ever do it's usually a LOL or LMAO to their offer and all messaging stops right then. In some cases, if the offer is stupid low I will either block their username or block their number so that I don't have to deal with them ever again. And they will never see any of my ads—so even better.

Scammers are the worst when it comes to texting. But they are easy to pick out. They usually want you to email them or they want to use a google call and will send you a code to put in to answer their call. It's always some guy in another country trying to pull a scam on you. Or you will get the generic BS where they say they will pay for your full asking price plus more if you ship the car to them. While it may look legit, they will send you a bad check (that looks real), but it will be a counterfeit when you try to cash it in at their bank or your bank. Don't fall for any of this! Only deal with people in person, or if through a text make sure it's a well-known company using its texting and email formatting. Don't even venture outside of wherever you have your car listed as it will then take away any protection you have using one of those sites. I have sold through eBay, Autotrader, CarGurus, etc. and I have never spoken to the person via phone or in person and I have had several successful transactions. So, there are legit people out there, but you'll know when you're dealing with a legit person or a scam person. If anything doesn't feel right, ask them for their number or give them yours and tell them to call you. Trust me, that person will call you (without a google call verification code).

The bottom line is, if you are not going through a valid car selling source and you are dealing with local buyers, I'd say 100% of your sales are going to be people who text or call you (NO EMAILS) and will ask you when you are available to show the vehicle. They won't ask you what's the lowest price, they won't go on and on about the vehicle's condition, they won't ask for the VIN number. They will want to set up a time to meet up and they will most likely buy the car if it's what they're looking for. Understand that banks are closed on the weekends and not a whole lot of people have all the money right there. But that is the gamble you'll have to consider. I'd say take it because I mostly sell to those people on Monday when the banks open back up. It's hard to pass on a good deal when people have been going to multiple cars that weekend and then they come across yours. It will be up to you if you want to take a deposit, but I usually don't. If they want it bad enough, they'll come back. Unless you're running a dealership and you can write them a receipt, then sure go ahead and take a deposit. That only ensures them to come back and complete the deal

Exception: The only time I will consider an offer through text is if the buyer is several hundred miles away. If they have to travel for over 3 hours or have to take a flight in, then I will entertain a text offer. While writing this book today I had a guy send me an offer and I agreed on the price. He drove for 6 hours, showed up and handed me the money. These are rare and people usually want to still negotiate on top of an agreed price. It will be up to you to determine that outcome. If anything, I will only agree to $100 off the asking price so they can get back home with gas. But we all know they have enough as they had the exact amount coming in. Some people I know would turn that person away even if they wanted $10 off. But I say what's a hundred if I'm just going to make more than a hundred on the next sale anyways. Everyone wants to feel they got a good deal at the end of the day.

Meeting people halfway to see your car

I am strongly against meeting people anywhere out of your way unless it's at your house, a place you are close to, a business you know, a police station (most have designated areas to do online business transaction now), a well-lit or crowded area or somewhere you are going to and could meet them on the way. But never go several miles or hours out of your way just to make a deal happen. I have had so many people tell me things like, "If it's like you say it is, I'll buy it on the spot," or "Can you just meet me halfway? It's a 2, 3 or even 5-hour drive for me." Here's the deal: if they are calling you it's because you have what they're looking for and you're one of the best prices out there (even if it is a 5-hour trip for them). They only want to meet you halfway in case it's something they don't want, then they only spend half the time getting to you. In general, the less a person has put into something physically, the less investment they're going to have into whatever they're looking at. When a person feels like they drove a long way, they're more open to making a few mistakes here and there. Plus, you should have the abundance mindset that more people are coming to see your car and you're not going to bend the rules for one person

Meeting people a long distance isn't that easy either. You have to find a friend available to follow you, in case you sell the car and now how are you going to get back? Going 2 hours out of the way isn't going to be a cheap

Lyft/ Uber ride back home. So, you'll have to find someone available at the time and day you need them. I've had to include some money to entice my friends to make the trip inconveniently. And if the other person doesn't want your car, you are now out of your time, wasted gas, and having to pay off your friend for the extra trip made.

I once had a guy drive 8 hours to my place because I refused to meet them halfway. When they showed up, they told me I was glad I didn't make the 4-hour trip to meet them because they would've turned me down. I met a person halfway once and they gave me $20 for gas, when it was over $50 to get to them. Sometimes if I have a place to be and it happens to be on the way, I will tell the buyer I can meet them halfway without telling them I'm actually in route in that direction anyways. I tell them I hope they plan on buying it because I am driving really far to meet them. This happened once and when I showed up, they didn't want the vehicle because it was missing a single air vent in the back of this SUV. A plastic vent that can be bought for $5 that didn't affect the a/c system or even the air back there was just ridiculous. I acted like they made me drive all the way out there but then I told them there was this body shop around the corner and I had to stop by there anyways. But I told the guy that if you ever tell someone to meet them halfway and they say no, it's because of people like you who ruin it for everyone else. That's why I stick to my rule if you really want to see my car, you'll find a way to get to me. If you don't then you weren't that serious anyways.

Does it change if they bought it offline and they have paid you the deposit and still want to meet you halfway? Suppose they say they'll pay for your gas. Nope the same rules still apply. I'll either meet someone at an airport free of charge, or they can Uber to my place once they've landed. They can set up a shipping transport or can come with a friend to pick it up. Trust me when I tell you, even the smoothest people will try to get you to come halfway. Those people might show up and if they find the littlest of things like let's say a rip in the carpet. You might think, really a rip in the carpet is what you're debating on from buying this car? The answer is yes, yes it will. And wouldn't it feel much better had you taken a few steps outside your house to get told this, instead of driving for hours to find this information out. I told you in other chapters to try and list everything as best as possible, but there will be instances where something small doesn't seem big to you, but to others it will. A tiny rock chip in the windshield you might not list, but to another person it's a deal breaker and they have to replace the whole windshield even if the rock chip is in the passenger side, at the very top not blocking anyone's visibility and will pass state inspection. Next time you'll question why you trusted the person and why you took their words: "I'll buy it; I just don't want to drive all the way out there" so seriously. My advice is don't do it! If you do, make sure it's going to be a cash deal. I mean what else is worse than driving that far? A person with a check trying to buy your vehicle

Where to buy parts

The most obvious place or known places are your local AutoZone, O'Rileys, NAPA, Walmart. These places provide instant parts and oil. If you need something right away and don't mind paying the 50% markup then it's okay to buy a part in a pinch. Sometimes none of these places will carry the part you need and only a dealership will have the part in stock. Dealerships will charge about 75 or even 100% mark up from the original price. I have had no other choice but to buy from a dealership when it comes to bolts, plastic fasteners, oil. But luckily, we have the internet and now we can buy from where these sources buy their parts from. That will be Amazon, eBay, Car-parts.com, Rock Auto. The key is to find the specific part number you need and then google search it to find the best deal on the net. Sometimes you have to go into a specific website and enter that part number to get the correct results. I find Rock Auto to be almost my go to online store (with a 5% online discount). Usually their parts come within 2-4 days.

Amazon and eBay are great sources to buy from as many dealerships and reliable car part places sell on these websites as well. The only downside is you have to wait until the seller ships your item.

Now Car-part is an interesting source. This is the place to buy used car parts. Mostly large parts like fenders, hoods, doors, suspension pieces etc. They have parts listed in either an A, B or C determining how much repair is needed to make the part original. A bumper might have a crack in it but repairable. A hood might have some light hail damage etc. Prices will vary from all the used car part stores online. Don't be afraid to buy out of state if that's your only choice. Call that store and ask them how much to ship to you. You can literally save hundreds of dollars buying from Car-part.com and the best part is most will be local in your area and you won't have to pay for shipping charges. Swing by and pick it up yourself. Carefully observe the item before you buy it! Some of these places only accept cash and their refunds can be sketchy.

Phone apps like Offer Up and 5 Mile are another backup source to look for a used part. You can negotiate the price with the seller if you think they are selling it too high. I have bought several parts off Offer Up. You get to meet really strange people there.

Craigslist is a good source to find local parts as well. Make sure you narrow down your search field and choose parts only. It's never a good idea to send offers over a text or call. Find out if the seller has it and plan to bargain in person. Never try and take off a $100, but be reasonable and try to talk them down $50 or so. If the price is really high, chances are the seller is not going to drop hundreds off, it's best to just move on. But if you want a laugh go ahead and see if you can offer a price over text and see what happens.

The last places are local junk yards. I have found that new parts can be a lot cheaper if you do some research and find one online. Otherwise you might have to travel with your tools to a junkyard to pull the parts off yourself. Junk yards are good for big items like motors, transmissions, large ext. body parts, specific OEM screws, frame pieces, tires etc. Pick-n-pull is a nation-wide junk yard that you can enter in your zip code and see if they have any vehicles you may need a part from. They even give you the arrival date. Most of the time, if it's a popular make and model and it's been there longer than three months chances of finding your specific wire or plug you may need it may be already gone. Only way to find out is to plan your day around a junk yard day.

Car part buying tip:

If you are looking at a car you might be interested in buying to flip and it needs some work done to it, my advice is to do a quick search on those items before you buy that vehicle. Sometimes a part you need may be back ordered or out of stock completely and the only source is one guy off eBay and he knows he's the only one who has the part you are looking for. That price may be a really stupid price too.

When to paint a car

Getting a good fresh paint job on any car is going to automatically boost your car's looks by 100%. The problem lies in the quality of the paint job. Over the years I have had my car professionally painted and not professionally painted by cutting corners in paint and body men. Going all out and paying over $1,500 or even $2,000 does nothing but help the buyer out in the long run. Getting a 5-year warranty or a 1-year warranty are basically the same thing when it comes to a flip. A buyer is going to judge the car on how it looks in person, they aren't worried about how long the paint is going to last at the time of purchase. Now maybe if you're buying a high-end car or perhaps a classic car then yes, these things will matter. Also, the price is going to be above normal than the regular cars you're selling for a quick flip. I have found that Earl Schibe and Maaco have been putting out good paint jobs that last over a year. I've seen videos on YouTube of people revisiting a Maaco paint job a year later and it still looks like the day it came out of the paint booth. Still shines with no paint flaking. The good thing about these paint shop corporations is that because their paint is cheap, their price is low. Now everybody hates these places because they'll complain about how long your paint job is going to last. I always tell them that I'm not trying to keep the car, but I'm trying to sell it. Small body shop people usually have prices starting at $1,200 and go up.

Body work is a different story. It's always the opposite when it comes to body work. The big corporations like Earl and Maaco will charge very high on the body work and the small shops will charge a lot less. So, what do I do? I get the body work done first at the small body shops and then take that car to a Maaco to get it painted. I save hundreds in the process using those two places against each other. The places I get the frame pulled, I will get a quote to fix anything I can't find like a dented trunk lid, hood, cracked bumper. I will just tell them to fix the repaired part, fill it with bondo and spray primer over it so all it needs to be is sanded once then it goes to the paint shop. Basic sanding at the paint shop is included in the paint. So, it works very well for both parties

Here is the thing when deciding to paint a whole car. First is, the original paint is going to last you up to 7-10 years. They use professional paint at the manufacturing plant when assembling the car. So, anything you have to paint over is going to lose that quality right off the bat. If you can put original paint in your sale, that alone goes a long way. If you can't, then you will be asked: "Where did you get the car painted?" Now let's say it's only a piece or two pieces that need to be painted. Well you can get a quote for those two pieces. It's usually a $200 minimum for all paint shops. So, it's something to consider depending on how much you got to budget for your car. Plus, the tricky thing is how hard it is to match your current car's paint. If your car has been sitting out in the sun for a long time, then obviously any new paint is going to look newer when taking pictures of the car, and your car will now stand out with those wrecked pieces being replaced. Sometimes it's easier for the painter to just paint the whole car, and when you start getting to needing 3 parts repainted then the price will be around $400, which a new paint job for the whole car might be around $600. I get my cars painted on a high scale level and my cost is $500 per car and $650 for an SUV. If I don't need one piece painted, I just paint the whole car. Even though I will ruin the original paint the outcome will flow instead of a few pieces standing out and making the car look like a repainted car than a brand-new paint job. White is the easiest to paint, it's easy to hide a lot of blemishes in the paint and body. Black is the hardest to paint because you can see every detail in the body and paint. Now a good painter can do a blend where they take the painted parts and then taper off an original part a quarter of the way to make it appear as an illusion and make it seem like it flows together. Again, it really depends on the paint color for this to happen. If the paint is a pearl, or a really exotic paint it will be hard for that painter to make it flow. You can ask them if they are able to do this or is it better to get a whole new paint job. That paint shop should tell you if it's possible or not

Runs in the paint, or some areas looking flat and not shining. This will depend on the body work done before your car was painted. Was it sanded down fully, was there an accident there and repaired and did the use enough paint? Runs in the paint or a dripping like motion in the paint is when a painter leaves the gun on while spraying into one area for too long therefore putting on more paint than needed and causing the paint to over layer and drip in paint. Once this is done it's nearly impossible to fix this in the moment. You'll have to wait until the paint dries and then sand that part down and try to buff it out. Sometimes it will require to be completely sanded down and repaint the whole area again. This will depend on the shop's credibility. Most shops will take ownership of their mistakes and will fix this for free. Some small shady shops will see this and not say anything to you hoping you never see it. Then one day when you have your car for sale a buyer will come buy and will point out how much of a crappy job the previous shop had painted your car. You can take your car back to that place and they may fix it for free, but are you going to want to do business with them again? Do you want to lose more time having to take something back after it's already listed? Do you want to get the same treatment of not noticing these things and them not telling you? I wouldn't and I would be looking for another paint shop ASAP! There are so many paint shops out there, that finding another one won't be hard to find.

A car is supposed to be shiny in all areas once it's been painted. There should be no flat spots where it isn't shiny. This is caused by places not being fully sanded down. You will most likely see swirl marks in the areas from the sander going over it and not fully getting the previous paint job completely off. If you see this, this is not normal. You should point this out to the shop owner and have them repaint that area. You are paying for a job and if the job is not 100% then you are not getting what you paid for. Buyers will notice these flaws, and if you can see it, so can they. Don't let your eyes fool you. Fix what needs to be fixed while your car is still at the paint shop. Accidents do happen and get overlooked, so don't blow up on someone's mistakes. If they make mistakes continually, then maybe you need to find another paint and body source

Rust is the cancer of all cars. You cannot paint over rust and not see the rust over the paint. Cars that sell up north or in snow areas go cheap for a reason. Salt on the roads eats up the body and paint on cars and will totally destroy the car's value. Not just body parts, but bolts, suspensions parts, mufflers, the frame etc. will all take the salt road abuse. When you are considering purchasing a car from up north consider that car most likely to have rust somewhere on the vehicle. Buying a car from up north and trying to sell it in a southern, western or even eastern county isn't going to fool anyone. Rust you cannot hide. When the rust sticks out people will automatically ask you if you bought it from up north. Then you will have a hard time selling that car. You have to try it once to see what the experience is all about. The prices are usually about $2,000 less than what you're used to buying, but it all comes back to you when you have to sell it for $2,000 less in the end.

Using multiple body shops and car mechanics

Never get settled in on one specific mechanic or body shop, trust me when I say this, things will sooner or later never go as you had planned. Dealing with numerous mechanics and body shop guys things will always start off cheap and your car will always take priority in their business. Here is the problem, once you start bringing them more cars, you would think that by bringing them business you two would be doing what businesses do and you both make money. Nope that will not be the case. Some body shop guys will even tell you straight up, hey I gave you a good deal at the beginning just to real you in, but only when things are starting to go south with that person is when their behavior comes out. I have known people who have known friends who grew up together etc. and even those relationships eventually go sour. Look people are human and we all have problems, the problem with that is some people don't know how to differentiate or know how to leave your personal problems at the door when you come to work. Those people will blow up on you and you may be a person who can handle these situations much better than I, but once a person does one thing once and they see you let that slide, they will eventually or will continue doing what they did because they see you have no problem with it. I on the other hand take the other approach and just leave and find a new source. It's sad to say but I usually have to find a new business place every year in the mechanical and body shop world. You see here is the thing, let's say things are working out and you've had no problems with a certain shop for the past 10 months, but you start to feel too comfortable with this person and you start to bring them more than one car. Now, you start to bring them 3 maybe 4 cars. Now you have multiple cars sitting at one location. The shop owner looks at this in three different ways. First is the good one and they are happy you are bringing them so much business (but that is the rare case). The second is they get jealous or envious of you because they see you making all this money and here, they are the ones putting in the manual labor and thinking they are only getting half or a quarter of what you're making. They will assume but never ask. Don't think by bringing them lunch will make their day. That will just amplify their beliefs. Also, don't ever under no circumstances tell them how much you've been making, how much you just made, or how much you are about to make. They shouldn't know anything about what you're doing except for the business you are bringing them. The last thing is, they think you are their only source and with the jealousy etc. they may not get to your cars as fast as they used to. In fact, your cars may be at a location for a very long time. Let's say you bring them a car, you've got all the parts for it, and then two weeks later they finally get to it. But just as they get to it, they tell you, you are missing a certain part. Then you check around for that part and realize that part is going to take X amount of days to get to you. You get that part then over the next few days they get to your car again and then tell you, you need another part, the cycle continues. It can get frustrating! I am good enough to determine that all parts a car needs before I even drop it off to a mechanic or body shop. I put all the parts inside the car and tell them, hey you got everything you need. But there are sometimes they still call me trying to get a delay and I will ask them which part and it's usually a common part and I'll bring it to them that day. Sometimes your car will be so wrecked even as a seasoned car flipper you won't know every little thing needed but you will try to get everything you know beforehand. You can ask that body guy or mechanic, but they will usually tell you, we won't know until we start removing parts. What does that mean, by now you should already know. That means when your car comes up and whatever time they feel like working on your car, they will find things to delay and move on to the next car. Yes, knowing that you better have other cars in other places because if you have 2 or more cars at one location your second car will not get touched until your first one is complete. You'd think they move on to your next vehicle but no that won't be the case. You might even ask them to look at your other car and they will make an excuse about getting your first car done etc. So again, this might draw frustration or you may handle it better than me but when a car has been at one location for over 2 months you start to question your instincts, and wonder what's really going on. Is it the body shop/ mechanic, the parts, the cars damage, you, etc. Blowing up on a person once you've reached your limit will get you nowhere. In fact, it will leave you in a worse position than you started. From all my past experiences when I finally call out a person about my car, there are usually some voices raised with the end result of the owner telling me to get all of my cars out of there. Then if you don't move them out at a certain time then he or she will start charging storage fees. This can get really tricky if you already gave the shop a deposit to start working on your car. Then you have to determine your refund etc. Going that route usually doesn't end well. And don't go home or come back a few days later with your tail between your legs because you've realized you have no other sources and try to let the owner have the upper hand and apologize for your outrage. Guess what? This will not change anything. Your cars will not take priority just because you had a heart to heart moment with a business partner. You just let them know they are still your only source.

There are so many benefits when you find a good body shop or mechanic. The prices start off cheaper than you've been dealing with. Your cars get done faster. The customer/owner relations are always in good spirits. But eventually, things will always have a kink in the situation, and it will test you mentally. My advice is to always be shopping around. Never bring more than one car to a person until they fix your first one. Never bring up prices or money to a shop regarding your income. Always let them know in subtle ways that you have other cars in other places by saying things like, hey when you remove that part put it aside because I got another car that needs that part in another location. Never be afraid to call out a shop owner on their steadily raising prices towards you. Those things might be funny at first but in time they won't. You may have to stop dealing with a shop for a while just so they recognize you're not falling for their bullshit prices. I've stopped dealing with shops and they call me months later asking if I'm still in business, and I just tell them yeah but are you going to start giving me good prices again because I'm getting your first prices you gave me elsewhere now. Usually, they will tell you to bring them a car and you'll talk business. But other times you might just have to cut off people and move on with your business. Sometimes those very same people will call you and you'll listen to them but you'll also remember what you experienced with them and when you hang up, you'll say yeah, I'm done with that situation.

If you are just starting off and you need to find some body shop and mechanics, I suggest you load up your car on a trailer and plan a day going to about 4 or 6 shops and get some estimates on your car. Taking pictures is never good enough to give to anyone. Everyone will tell you to bring the car in. But you don't want to get some low estimate and then line up a tow truck, pay the tow truck fees only to find out that the low price was a phone quote and the real price is much higher. Look under Craigslist under car repair, body shops, mechanics. and call them and talk to them. Make sure they have an actual shop and not working out of their backyard. Believe me some people will say they paint and not even have a paint booth and will literally paint your car in the back yard with no tarp or anything. You can imagine the results of that when you pick it up. And yes, I have been there, lol. Also look at Offer Up or body shops or mechanics in your area in Google Maps and see if they are surrounded by more mechanics in that area. Usually, they will be in the most industrial areas. But even if they are not listed, doesn't mean they don't do good work. They might have the resources to advertise and may be the very shops you are looking for. They are hungry for business and here you come with all this work to do. You'd be amazed to know that some of these small shops are unlisted and are constantly busy. However, you can talk with them and find out why they only work for one or two car dealers. Those dealers will bring them 2 or 3 cars per week and will punish them if they do work on other people's cars in their shop. Yeah, you read that right. "How?" you ask. Simple: the dealers know they have other workers wanting their business and one mishap will cause that shop to lose their weekly salary. Don't be mad at the dealer, that's where you want to be. When I first heard that that only energized me to know that someone has the sole power and confidence that one place will take care of them only. Starting off you will experience what I am telling you now. You are not some big dealer and people will treat you as such. But you got to get your feet wet and knowing basic business relations is where it all starts. Getting to know how long things take, what the normal prices are, and knowing when you're getting screwed. So, if anything, don't put all of your eggs in one basket. Divide them up. See how other people work vs other shops. You will be treated differently at every location. So, get ready and know this is all a part of the car flipping game.

Working with auto transport companies

In this business it's hard not to look outside your city for other opportunities. Maybe you wondered about buying a vehicle through eBay or Autotrader but didn't feel up to the dishonesty about a seller's feedback, or description. While most of these websites offer guarantee, nothing is ever safe. But then again, is anything ever safe even when you buy from a local auction? Nope. Everything in this business is based on reputation and feedback. I'd say once you have bought from cities far away, you'll quickly notice why those vehicles at that spot will go higher than others. Why? Because that city maintenance crew really knows how to keep their cars in check and when you get them, they are extremely well taken care of. Sometimes you might have to venture outside of those places to find even better deals. This is where auto shippers come into play

On eBay you will have the generic UShip. Now let me be clear when I tell you this, everyone that transports uses some sort of broker to ship your car. UShip along with several other companies that will post Tractor Trailer or Semi-Trucks with car haulers showing they ship all kinds of cars everywhere. But not one of these companies are the shipper themselves. They are all called brokers. They all use a software called Dispatch. Dispatch is what the actual shipping companies use to see what cars are going where and how much you are willing to pay.

Just because you use a well-known Broker aka Auto Shipper, doesn't mean you're going to get a more quality care, or a faster response. Most of the auto shippers avoid the big companies because they have had several bad experiences with them. You see a big company would rather burn a small transport driver/ company to appease a customer. After a while, no drivers want to work for them. When money is lost, or something was promised and not received these guys get upset mainly due to not being in the conversation between the broker and the customer. All the driver does is pick up their car and deliver it to wherever it needs to go.

The way a broker works (depending on who you work with) will find out the local rates and then decide what profit they want to make off you. As an example, suppose your car cost $600 to ship. The broker determines the distance and what the going rate a driver charges, it may be something like .25 cents a mile. But they will never tell you this information because the less you know the better for them. So, they will tell you that to move your car the rate is $1,000. When it's really only $600 (with the miles being X). The $400 is what the broker wants to make off you. They will call it their broker fee. I mean literally, they can charge you anything they want.

The way quotes work: If you were to type in Instant Auto Shipping Quotes in google you will get several companies offering 3,5,10 instant quotes once you put in your vehicle/ distance information. I highly suggest you create a new email account for this, and possibly a fake number as you will get quotes for the next month almost on a daily basis. You will also get several calls if you put your actual number in. Don't put in your real number and only call the companies that are giving you the lowest quotes. You will see all kinds of price ranges. If you were to take my previous example of the $600 quote, you will get quotes from $300 - $1,400. Again, paying more doesn't put you in a higher priority or with a better company. They might be able to put in a higher starting price for a driver to notice your car more, but any company can do this. So if you were to find a company willing to charge you $600 + a $100 broker fee then you could ask them if you could add an additional $50 to set yours above everyone else (if you really needed it picked up sooner than later) Paying the lowest, or even calling those people back is only going to leave you frustrated in the end. These people just want your business and will do anything to get a phone call. If you do call them, expect your quote to be higher than the low quote you received. They will tell you some BS story about you didn't enter this in, or due to the distance, miles etc. and will try to convince you it's just a standard thing everyone goes through. The worst is if they say it is that low price and tell you they need a deposit in the amount of X until they can get a driver out there, you will end up paying and never hear from them again. They may call you, or you may end up calling them out of frustration and they will tell you they had several drivers out there but nobody could pick up your vehicle due to the position it's in. But they will say they found one driver, but he wants more money to pick it up. Is this story even true at this point? I have had some many friends and heard of so many people getting ripped off in the Auto Shipper world. So how do you find a good one? Let's discuss…

Finding a reputable auto shipping company. An honest broker is going to tell you the going rates from point A to B. They are going to tell you the miles a driver gets on that route. They will tell you the exact shipping quote and then tell you how much they charge. I've had good people charge me $50 per car and some $100 per car. Usually when I have to search for a new Auto Shipper a good one will start me out at $150 per car and when they see me buying several cars per month (and using their services) they will drop it down to $100 per car. I would never pay $200, $250 or even $300 per car. That to me is just highway robbery. I mean seriously, you expect me to pay a ridiculous fee just because you have a broker license to ship cars and sit behind a desk and just do a couple of clicks? Not when all of their business is generated through people calling them. This isn't the stock market where you're making calls to get the good tips for the day.

Beating the system: If you ever want to avoid paying the broker fee, all you have to do is acquire an auto dealers license. The software company Dispatch can authorize you as a car dealer and you can put in your own info into this software and get your own rates. You will have to deal with these drivers directly, but you will be saving money. If you are bilingual, it's a plus because a lot of these drivers are foreigners and don't speak good English. Sometimes if you quote a price too cheap, the driver may call you to discuss a higher payment since they'll be in your area. It will be up to you to determine that outcome. It really isn't necessary to be a member of Dispatch just to get into this game. I am just giving you options on things to consider down the road. I actually like dealing with my broker because they take my load off the shipping thing for $100 and all I give them is my car info and where it's to be picked up and dropped off. I give them the time, the place, the hours of operation and a contact number to call. I get all of this info once I've won a vehicle from that auction company. When there are mishaps in the shipping my broker handles everything and just updates me on everything. It really reduces the stress on the shipping. The last thing I need is a driver telling me what cars they need to pick up, where they're going, which car is it, weather delays etc. It can be exhausting when you're mainly focusing on sales and inventory etc.

The way a driver works: I'd figure I'd throw this in there just to give you an idea what the driver sees when they consider picking up your vehicle. First as they are starting their day off, or it's night and they are planning things for tomorrow, they will log into Dispatch and see what type of cars are in their area and where they are going. If they can pick up 3 and are going to a general area on the way, it's something to consider for them. If it's one car, then they will expect a higher pay. But if they have no work then that one car is actually a job for them to do without negotiating the price. If your car is considered an In-op meaning in operational, then it's definitely something they will have to consider. Does it roll? Will they need a winch to pull it onto their trailer? A lot of drivers don't have wenches on their trailers. Only the 3 car haulers will have a winch on their trailer. Most of the big runners with the dual stack trailers are only good for running cars. If they can have a forklift put it onto their truck, they can possibly move it, but this is something they will call your broker about. Your broker may call you, and you can either call the place or the broker can call them to find out. The driver will not have the pick-up information nor a contact person so they can't call the place themselves. It sometimes works out and they can put your car at the end of the trailer so it's the first one off. But if they have to put your car at the front of the trailer then they will not be able to get it on. Not even a forklift can go that high. So, to sum it up, if you bought a car more than 1,000 miles away, and it's another 3 hours from any major city, don't expect a 3-car hauler to make that trip. Anything over 1,000 miles is for those big semis with the double stack trailer (5 cars on top and 5 cars on bottom). You might get lucky and find a car hauler that somehow is going in your direction but expect to pay about $300 more than your quoted price. You'll pay it when your car hasn't had any responses in the past 30 days. It's something to consider when purchasing a car far away. A lot of auctions will have a map to determine the location of the vehicle from your spot. If the car runs, you're in a lot better shape than a car with a blown engine but rolls.

If the driver agrees on the price that pays, they will call to confirm the pickup hours etc. and the broker will dispatch that ticket to them. Once this is done nobody else can call the broker until that driver releases it. The only reason they'll release it is due to a problem with the vehicle. Such as it's a non-runner when told it was a runner. Or a wheel is missing, or the vehicle is in a spot they can't get to. They'll call the broker with their frustration/ concerns and will explain to you the situation. An option may be to hire a local tow truck to get it on the trailer. It most cost you another $50-$75 just for the tow truck. That will be added to the quote when the driver drops off your car. So, if everything goes smooth and the driver is able to load your vehicle onto their trailer then they will mark the vehicle as Picked up on Dispatch. Now you sit back and wait for your car to show up. The broker will give you the drivers info in case you need to call them. Payment is usually C.O.D cash on delivery and sometimes a Money Order. Never checks or a credit card.

The driver will mark all the noted discrepancies/ faults/ scratches/ dents etc. when they pick up the vehicle. It will be your responsibility to double check what they wrote there before and after it is delivered. I've never had any unknown issues arise when delivered. I've had a few surprises that the auction had pulled after taking pictures of the car being sold, and I once had a hydraulic shock on a driver's trailer go bad and spewed oil on all of the cars behind it. It was no biggie that a car wash couldn't take off. I had one instance where a driver said he was going to be here on a certain day and then showed up 4 days later. The only thing was I was 2 hours away when you sent me a text saying HERE! Then his wife called me about 30 times asking when I was going to be there the whole 2 hours to get there. It wasn't good, lol. But for the most part I've had good experiences with auto transport drivers. When you come across a good transport driver you can always ask for their information if you plan on buying more vehicles from that location. They'll tell you to call them direct and get the same quote minus the broker fee. It will be your little inside trading. No harm no foul. We're all here to get a better deal when we find one.

Overhead Hiring and Being your own Boss

You can save a lot of money the more you know how to fix your own cars. The problem becomes when you have several cars that need work and you are a one-man business. Sometimes these situations can become overwhelming and can be depressing at times. You might be waiting on a part to arrive, one car you might not be able to figure out the problem, one might need more body work than hand tools can fix. One car must go to this shop, but this shop is too full to take in any new cars. When you have too many cars to deal with, and not enough resources to fix them, it can become overwhelming. Therefore, you either need to A) not buy so many cars (which is hard to do) or B) find help or hire help to help your business flow. When I say hire, I mean subcontract your work out. Find a body shop, mechanic and mobile mechanic to help things go faster.

The way I look at my business model I subcontract all my work out to individual shops. It is my responsibility to get my cars to each location. I pay that person to do one job and then I move it to the next. I rarely let one shop do everything. I've done that in the past and that shop always wants to jack up the price eventually when giving you a quote for their specialty instead of a roundabout to fix everything. So, instead of asking for quotes (for example, "How much to fix everything?"), only ask them their specific specialty (for example, "How much just to straighten out the frame?"). The problem is their one specialty starts to get higher as time goes on. Not because they are raising their prices on you, but because they got used to the extra money and now don't want to go back to being paid in a smaller amount. So, to make up for the fake inflation, they will try to keep the once normal price a higher markup. So, try not to have one place do everything as this becomes a custom too easily.

Finding people who know how to do one specific skill can save you time and money. When it comes to dropping a car off at one location, you want one person doing one thing so they can see your car as an easy project. When you have a list of things to do, your car will sit there for a while until all the cars that need the quick fixes are out of the way. Then when it comes to work on your car something always comes up like a needed part, and you're sitting there thinking why wasn't this mentioned or looked at earlier? The car had already been there two weeks and you're just now letting me know this? I could've already ordered it online and gotten it much cheaper, but now I am forced to go buy it at a local part store and the markup will be 50-80% higher. The situation never gets any easier when you bring that one location with more cars because they will look at it like you didn't seem to care how long they took to get to your first car and now you're bringing them another car? Expect your cars to take longer each time you bring them one. It's not until they finish one should you be bringing them more. Of course, they will tell you to bring them more work but only because they want to have money sitting there waiting for them. Who wants an empty shop not generating any business? While they got their work lined up, you're now on their waiting list. I know a lot of people reading this won't follow my advice, but you must experience these things to understand what I'm talking about. In this business it's hard to find honest people. Everything starts off great then things get normalized and that person's true behaviors come out. It usually falls on the lazy end filled with lies and broken promises.

Flipping cars can start off as a hobby and quickly turn into a profitable business. When you must start thinking about renting or buying a shop, then you'll have to think about W2 and 1090 forms. Hiring maybe a full or part time mechanic, a body shop helper, or a body man. Owning your own shop with your own staff that knows how to work on cars is where we all want to be. Getting there can take years, but it is obtainable. Easier than most people think. Some start-up shops that can store two cars can be found for about $500 a month. This shop won't have a shower— it may not even be livable—but it is something to get your business up and running on a more serious level. Most banks can handle employee payroll and direct deposits. You can find several online payroll accounts, software to track employee timecards, and several online catalogs to buy punch in clock equipment or log in software.

Once you get into the hiring phase, you can start looking into getting a bank loan. Although most banks will want a 2-3-year tax record to determine if your business is a profitable business or a hobby. But having employees at your establishment, having good credit are some key points to getting a large loan. When you have payroll to keep up, a lease you're paying on, and an investment coming in they will see you as an established company.

Trying to get a $50,000 loan on a business is not like getting a loan for a $50,000 car. The car is tangible and can be taken back and sold for recovered loss. Getting a loan is intangible and something they cannot repossess. So, handing you out even something small as $20,000 is a big deal to a bank. We are talking about getting a $200k or $300,000 loan. Something to get really started. Even at 300k you still need to buy shop tools and you won't even be able to buy 50% of what you really need. But as time goes on, you'll acquire all the things you need. Basic things like an air compressor, air tools, sockets, wrenches, floor jacks, toolboxes are what you'll need. Car lifts, frame straighteners etc. will come in time. This is on a bigger scale but eventually it's where you want to be. There's nothing better than coming up the ranks of car flipping. Grinding and learning all of the mistakes, mishaps, and learning curves is how you'll come to be successful in this business. You have to fail a little to learn a lot. Without failure there are no greater rewards.

How does this sound, you wake up and log on to see all the auctions for the day or the week? You do your searches for all the cars you're interested in, you either save or watch those for future bidding. You may even have to attend a few online auctions for the day. You check to see where your parts are in the shipping process to get to you. You schedule your routes to go and check up on your car's progress and see if any of the shops you're working with need anything from you. You come home because you have to clean and list a car that you got yesterday. You have people texting you and calling you about the cars you have posted. This is your day to day job now. Scheduling car transports, finding the cheapest used parts, buying the greatest deals and having other people work on your cars for you. Maybe some small jobs you can do yourself and you put on some earbuds and listen to your favorite music while you install a new radio or add some new wipers. Daily traffic is no longer a part of your life. Having to be accounted for somewhere instead of being marked late is no longer your priority each morning. Job meetings, quarterly job performances, wearing a certain clothing attire are all out the window now. You are your own boss. You are the creator of your own income. Any failures and profits are now up to you. There are no excuses. The only excuse you should be asking is why haven't I thought of this sooner. I feel the person reading this has good intentions and can imagine themselves running such a business. You know you are right for this if you picked this book up. You know you'll have the know how to get things going pretty quickly. The only thing is when are you going to start?

TT&L – knowing state and local laws

Tax title and license

When I sell cars, I am not a dealer and I will tell every buyer that the TT&L will be up to them and their state they register it in. I sell my cars without official license plates and sell all of my cars with a temporary paper tag/ plate. Depending on your state they may offer a 24, 72 hours, 30, 60- or 90-day temporary tag. You can either buy them directly off the states auto registry online or you might have to go in person to buy one. Where I live now they have toll roads and if you ever sell a car with a legit license plate or paper plate and you don't let the state know you no longer own that car, the next person can run up toll charges and all those bills will be sent to you (because it's still legally under your name if the new buyer hasn't registered the vehicle yet). If people ever ask me where the plate is, I tell them I sell it with a paper plate. If they ever give me any grief about needing a regular plate or they won't buy it then my dealings end with them. Because from what I just told you they are trying to use your plate with your name attached to it, most likely due to warrants and don't want a car registered under their name. Either way I sell my cars legit. It may only be temporary but at least I can get the buyer home legally. It is up to them who's name they want to put it under, who's insurance, and if they even want to register it or not. I am just here to sell cars, I am not involved in the title license dept. If you ever want to become a dealer then the state authorizes you to handle the exact same responsibilities the state does. You basically become a title and registry department when you become a dealer.

As much as I love to sell without a dealer's license there comes a time when one must face the legal side of things in this business. Each and every state will let you sell a certain amount before you have to register for a used car dealer license. Selling over the state limit can come with consequences. I was once involved selling over the state limit by 3 cars. I was never doing anything out of the ordinary, it was a guy I sold a car to and he went to 3 different locations thinking he could get a better tax deal or something to that effect. He went to so many title places he drew a red flag on himself. And when he finally went to his last place, he couldn't even register it. Then he started claiming he bought a stolen car to the title place and then that drew the state troopers in. That was how I got tracked down and that's why I was caught. I knew what I was doing, and even though I was paying the state tax on all of my vehicles when I went to get my titles done, I knew I was on the illegal side. The thing was I had my dealers license up to a certain point but due to me only selling less than 10 cars a year at that time and the state requiring a license selling past 7 at first, I got into the whole license thing. It started off as a hobby for me and I was always following the rules. Until I saw renewing the dealer's license outweighed the individual flipping, I thought I would just stick to the individual unless I saw a real growth potential to require a dealer's license again. I guess I went by the book first when I should've tried things in reversal. But that is my story, you can decide how you want to start off in this industry and what your state laws require. Some states never check on this kind of stuff. The same state I was in I had known of people flipping 50+ cars without being hassled by the state, it was just my bad luck that I had to be set an example of. When I had gone to court for that I ended up having to pay a $1,000 per car for every car I sold past the legal limit. That wasn't even the profit I had made on some of those cars. Plus, I already paid for the state taxes on the car when transferring the title. Again, I was a small fish in the pond, but I learned my lesson. You never know what's going to happen when you pass the state laws of their selling limit without a dealer's license.

If you ever want to make this a career and you do want to get a dealer's license, then you'll have to look up your state's requirements. You may have to rent a location that subsides or zones in a car sales area. You may have to get a business phone number, Signs of your business name, hours of operation, a certain number of cars that can be stored on premises, you might even have to get insurance bonded. A bond means you have insurance for drivers if they got in an accident while test driving. Depending on how good your credit is, you might have to pay anywhere between $500-$5,000. You'll have to pick a business name, register that business name, it's optional but if you've gone this far you should get a domain name with your business name in it. It may sound daunting to require all of this but there are a lot of people who profit from startups like this (body shop rentals, mechanic shops, etc.). I would look on Craigslist for example and look up used car lots in the housing dept. You should find some landowners who are zoned in the right area you need and have several small shops that you can rent for about $500 to get you up and running. It will have all the state requirements you need to pass. These will be run down shops as several entrepreneurs have tried to have a go in the car flipping world. Some move on to bigger shops as they evolve, others use that shop for about 3-5 years. Some will come and go. But I suggest if you're serious about getting into the car dealership industry, I suggest getting one of these small startup/ front shops to see if it's something you want to get into. I don't recommend you spend $2,500 on a big shop that holds up to 10 cars and is off a busy road. You might be working just to pay off bills. So, do what others do, start off with a small location. Use your house or a friend's house to store the other cars you have until you get a big enough business going so you can branch out to bigger and better places. People need cars every day! No matter how many people get into this game, there is always a need.

Curb stoning. This is what the state would like to describe your business once you have passed the legal limit of car selling. They will describe you as ripping people off on the side of the road without a proper business license. Even if you may be selling some really good cars with some of the best deals out there, if the state isn't aware of your transactions, they will label you as such. Dealers hate it because they have to follow the rules and you don't. But it's not like you're making all this amazing money doing so. You're just cutting the paperwork and not giving the state their share of taxes on each sale. Here's how it works. Let's say you bought a car for $1,000 and you paid the state sales tax of 10% (this is just an example). The state only gets $100 from you from your purchase. Then you sell it for a profit, but the state doesn't know if you made a profit or had a loss without having paperwork to send in to them about your progress. If it's a loss, nobody wins, but if it's a profit then that's where the state wants to kick in. This is why being a used car dealer follows a different set of rules. A dealer won't have to pay state taxes and will be tax exempt. But the state will gain a higher tax bracket when the dealer sells it for a higher price than what they bought it for. I mean why would you be in a business if you're not making a profit or income? So, back to an individual, suppose you sell a car for $5,000 only having to put in an additional $1,000 to fix it you've made a $3,000 profit. But the state will never know of your profits. When the buyer goes in to transfer the title, he can say he paid $1,000 for it. The state will make another $100 of the next buyer but that's not what they want. They want sellers to make a higher profit and document the new higher selling price. So, if it's the $5,000 as previously noted, with the same deduction of $1,000 in repairs, the profit is still the same for you, but now the state gets to charge a higher tax rate. So now the tax rate is $5,000 + 10% state tax. So instead of the buyer paying the $100, they are now forced to pay the new $500. This is why the state hates individual car flippers. This is why car flippers without a dealer's license are called curb stoners. The state always wants a piece of the pie. Trust me I know! They wanted $1,000 per car for each car I sold over the legal limit and that was pretty steep. Luckily, I had a cool judge that day and said if I had $500 to cover the costs, he would dismiss the charges. I agreed, paid, and life went on. Don't be me, lol. There may be legal consequences whenever you live. It's best to know these once you reach the 3-car selling point.

Truth be told

I have to create a topic just for this one purpose. I may have explained it here and there in this book, but I want to make this a center point and quite frankly one of the last pieces of this puzzle. It is, once you have mastered the game of the car flipping industry there comes a point when you have to walk a customer. What do I mean? You see when you work for a big car corporation you are working under their umbrella. You can't go off on a customer or you'll get fired. You can't walk a customer without getting a manager involved (who outranks your position) to see if they can get the customer to agree to a deal. Everything involves kissing the ass of the consumer. Everyone at a big dealership works for a paycheck, and everyone will get written up or fired if they don't try to appease the customer in every way possible. Most customers who have bought cars from a big dealer know this hierarchy in this chain and will either want to speak to the manager directly to cut out the salesman or will wait it out to act like the company is getting the best of them when in actuality they know the process and use their own terms against them (without being so specific).

When you are running your own ship, you get to make all the calls. You determine the starting price; you determine the final selling price. You do all the negotiating and handle all the traffic. You are responsible for all the ads, the fees, the description, the time to set aside. After all is said and done and you have worked with the body shop guys, the mechanical guys, the transmission shops, the electrical shops, it is time to sell your vehicle. Knowing everything you got the car to be in its best condition to resale you have to know your market. Once you know that your car is at the top 3 of cars with the best miles, condition and price you will have a lot of people who will say they can get better than yours. But the truth is they don't. Some are looking for a quick flip themselves off your time and energy. Some just want to see if you will go lower just because they asked. This is where you have to be upfront and honest. Sometimes you have to be downright rude to get your message across.

If someone were to message you an absurd price, like $3,000 off your asking price, I don't know about you but that is insulting to me. I specifically put any low ballers get discarded in my ads as a warning, but some people won't even read that part. Maybe they do and just don't care anyways. But if you ever find yourself in a position where a person wants to lowball you and you continue the conversation with them, trust me when I say this, no matter what price you come up with over text, they will still try to lowball you once they show up in person. I usually tell them, hey the price is the price so if you don't come up here with X amount, we agreed to, you're just wasting your own time. Still they will try and if not, they will not buy. I can't tell you how many times people will show up and then try to talk me down even after I told them not to show up without the full amount otherwise and yet they still try.

There have been times where I will just shut the car off before they want to pop the hood or take it for a test drive and I'll tell them the deal is off and I will just walk away.

Some people who don't know about cars will bring a friend that knows a little and usually it will be their downfall. Again, when you know your car and you know the market, yet you have some yahoo come in telling you they hear a motor issue, or something about the paint, the interior etc., it's time to cut them off and walk away. You will feel better about yourself than to hear someone who doesn't know what they are talking about telling you all the things wrong about your car. There could be nothing wrong with your car, it's been checked out thoroughly by a top mechanic and yet someone who wants to lowball you will try to point out non existing things just to get it cheaper. With me, they will fail. I will shut down any current conversation, turn the car off and tell them this isn't the car for you and will walk away. They will stand there in shock, but I didn't come here with some junior mechanic trying to trash talk my car to get a few hundred bucks off. Sometimes when people play hardball with me, I will tell them I got a few more people stopping by to look at it for the price I'm going to sell it to them without trying to knock it down lower. Sometimes those people will drive away and then call me 5 min later telling me they're coming back to get it. Or they could ask me, "This is your best offer?" In this case, I would say yes and then they go back to their car to see if a friend could let them borrow X amount of dollars until they get paid again. It's usually just a front and they had the money the whole time.

Imagine a person low balls you in person, you tell them to call you when you get all the money and the very next person who shows up gives you the full asking price without negotiating? Do you think you'll feel stupid for almost giving your car away for zero profit or feel thankful knowing you stuck to your guns and waiting for a better price?

I've turned away people who've walked up and said, boy that's a bad paint job. I return by saying, "Well, that's all I needed to hear. You have a good day." Then, I walk right back to where I came from. I've walked up to meet some people and they have said, it's not exactly what I was looking for and I just turn around without saying a word. When someone says the littlest things it's my cue, they want a super cheap price. I have been on this flip side where I have tried to work with these people in the past. Nodding my head about a scratch here, a small dent there, a crack here, or a chip there. It's small things that the customer will say they need to fix but in reality, they aren't going to do a damn thing about it. Now if my car is marked up high, then sure let's negotiate. But when it's marked super low, there is no wiggle room. I mean when you really want to blast out a car there is no need to start losing money just for the sake of cause. You are not in the business to lose money. I don't care even if you have to break even to learn a lesson, at least you are breaking even. But to lose money is not what this business is about.

The only time I have lost money is when I am at the point where I am going to make the sale just to break even and then a mechanical issue pops up after driving it for over a hundred miles etc. Like say the tranny starts to slip, or you blow a tire, and you need a noticeable repair. The more you drive a car the more you will have chances of things going wrong. It doesn't happen often, but it does, and you just have to deal with those situations. But what I am talking about is when your car is in top shape and you have it at the best price, don't fall for the low ballers. Sometimes you can't tell over a text or phone call. You just have to experience it in person. Don't be afraid to walk a person. Someone out there wants your car for the price you're asking for, so make sure that you know where your car sits in the market.

Truth be told, not every car deal is going to go smoothly. Sometimes you'll have to mentally or verbally tell people, "Have a nice day" and then walk away.